LEADERSHIP GEMS IN THE BIBLE
(THE OLD TESTAMENT VOL. 1)

LEADERSHIP GEMS IN THE BIBLE

THE OLD TESTAMENT

- Volume 1 -

CHRIS OMOIJIADE

Scribe Tribe
www.scribetribe.media

Furthermore, the publisher does not have control over and does not assume any responsibility for author or third-party websites or their content.

unless otherwise indicated, all Scripture quotations were taking from THE KING JAMES VERSION of the Bible.

Scripture quotations noted NIV are from The Holy Bible, NEW INTERNATION VERSION.

Scripture quotations noted NLT are from The Holy Bible, NEW LIVING TRANSLATION.

Scripture quotations noted ESV are from The Holy Bible, ENGLISH STANDARD VERSION.

Published by:
ScribeTribe Africa
The Scribe Place,
Brownstone Estate,
Lekki, Lagos

www.scribetribe.media
scribetribeafrica@gmail.com
+234 708 040 1080, +234 813 527 3602

Distributed by:
The Chris Omoijiade Company
+234 810 950 0000, +234 908 123 0000
ceo@tcocglobal.com
admin@tcocglobal.com
www.tcocglobal.com
chrisomoijiade
Chris Omoijiade
Christopher Omoijiade
Christopher Omoijiade

THE
Chris Omoijiade
COMPANY
SOLI DEO GLORIA

CHRISTOPHER E. OMOIJIADE
SOLI DEO GLORIA

ARIMATHEA
ARIMATHEA BELIEVERS NETWORK

*This book is dedicated to Yahweh,
the I Am, the Holy Father of all spirits
and heavenly lights.*

*To Jesus the Christ, Prince of Peace,
the Word and Eternal King.*

*And the indispensable
Sceptre of the living Sovereign God,
Spirit of Glory, Wisdom and Revelation,
the Holy Spirit.*

*I am indeed a product of
undeserved mercy.*

*Thank you, Abba, for
adopting me!*

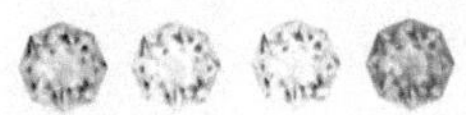

CONTENTS

LEVITICUS

NUMBERS

TABLE OF CONTENTS

DEUTERONOMY

JOSHUA

JUDGES

RUTH

I SAMUEL

TABLE OF CONTENTS

II SAMUEL

I KINGS

II KINGS

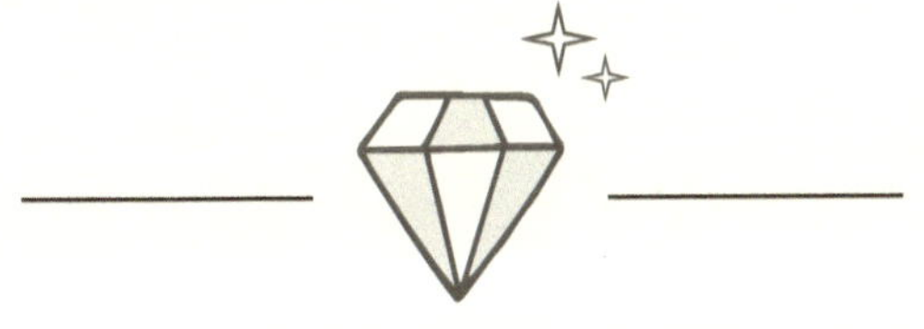

THE BOOK OF
GENESIS

- 💎 1 -

TACTFUL IN HANDLING
SENSITIVE DISPUTES

*"Then the Lord said to Cain, "Why are you angry?
Why is your face downcast? If you do what is right,
will you not be accepted? But if you do not do what is
right, sin is crouching at your door; it desires to have
you, but you must rule over it."*
—*Genesis 4:6, 7, NIV*

One of the examples of the earliest gems in the first book of
the Bible, in my opinion, is tact as shown by God himself,
the very source of all we need to learn about leadership. The
skill and sensitivity displayed are worthy of consideration
by any god-fearing leader. Here, we find the children of
the progenitors of the human race both making an offering
to the Lord. Cain, who worked the soil, brought some of
the fruits of the soil, and his brother Abel also brought
an offering—fat portions from some of the firstborn of his
flock.

God looked down on both offerings and expressed with
tact His approval for one, and disapproval for the other.
In addressing Cain, you can feel the emotional dexterity in
His words. Though displeased he started off speaking to
why His anger was all over the place, and understanding
that in such a scenario the next emotion that will prop up
will be something more disastrous, offering him a leeway

of redemption whilst reminding him of a possible negative outcome.

Leaders, when speaking, must always be conscious of the power of their spoken words to either build up or potentially pull people down. In situations when multiple parties are involved, there is an extra layer of tact brought to the fore. Godly leaders are not brash and should be able to hide their iron hands in velvet gloves to avoid alienating those they lead.

- 💎 2 -

PREPARATION

"When Abram heard that his relative had been taken captive, he called out the 318 trained men born in his household and went in pursuit as far as Dan. During the night Abram divided his men to attack them and he routed them, pursuing them as far as Hobah, north of Damascus. He recovered all the goods and brought back his relative Lot and his possessions, together with the women and the other people. After Abram returned from defeating Kedorlaomer and the kings allied with him, the king of Sodom came out to meet him in the Valley of Shaveh (that is, the King's Valley). Then Melchizedek king of Salem brought out bread and wine. He was priest of God Most High, and he blessed Abram, saying, "Blessed be Abram by God Most High, Creator of heaven and earth. And praise be to God Most High, who delivered your enemies into your hand." Then Abram gave him a tenth of everything. I will accept nothing but what my men have eaten and the share that belongs to the men who went with me—to Aner, Eshkol and Mamre. Let them have their share."
—Genesis 14:14-20, 24, NIV

Abraham (Abram at the time) was the first to highlight an important gem found in the scripture, which was the art of preparation. The patriarch, whose influence crisscrosses the major religions of our age, received some unwelcoming news from a distant land about the kidnapping of his relative Lot, his family and possessions. Anyone who has found themselves in such an uncomfortable situation knows that time is of the essence when acting; otherwise, with every tick of the clock, the probability of recovery dwindles significantly.

Abraham had an army of 318 men who were trained (for a man who was on the move from Ur of the Chaldeans to his place of promise, intelligence dictates he must have invested in a security architecture to protect his movement), and together with them pursued the marauders by leading a night surprise attack that gave him a victory of important proportion—it was just after this victory that he had the encounter with Melchizedek (the King of Salem who had no genealogy) to celebrate the victory, opening a new chapter with his walk with God all borne from his preparation.

As a godly leader, are you prepared? While it may be inconceivable to be prepared for virtually all scenarios that may confront your leadership, possessing a mindset of preparation is a vital key for every leader to attain true and lasting success. Leaders must always be in a preparatory mode.

- ◆ 3 -

HOSPITABLE

"He said, "If I have found favor in your eyes, my Lord, do not pass your servant by. Let a little water be brought, and then you may all wash your feet and rest under this tree. Let me get you something to eat, so you can be refreshed and then go on your way— now that you have come to your servant." "Very well," they answered, "do as you say."
—*Genesis 18:18i, NIV*

In my over two decades of interaction with leaders from every walk of life and across the entire spectrum of leadership, I am yet to find a truly successful leader who failed in this department. Leaders worth copying are usually driven by a spirit of hospitality.

Here we have father Abraham sitting near the great oak trees of Mamre in what must have been a very hot afternoon in a place not too far from Hebron. He looks up and sees three men standing nearby; under no obligation, he hurries out to meet them and even bows low to the ground.

Like every godly leader should do, he requests that water be brought to refresh the men (who were heavenly messengers), and instructs his wife to knead the finest flour for bread and picks the best choice, tender calf (not the one about to give up the ghost), along with curds and milk.

This encounter was the precursor to the prophetic age-long prayer request for a child. His hospitality, though not specifically stated, can be assumed. Isaac was prophesied, and not only that, the Lord revealed his mission to destroy Sodom, which triggered intercession by Abraham.

How many angels have probably walked by you without a second glance? Remember the Bible says some have unknowingly attended to angels. Godly leaders cannot resist being hospitable to fellow human beings.

- ◈ 4 -

BUILDING ON PAST SUCCESSES

"So Isaac moved away from there and encamped in the Valley of Gerar, where he settled. Isaac reopened the wells that had been dug in the time of his father Abraham, which the Philistines had stopped up after Abraham died, and he gave them the same names his father had given them."
—Genesis 26:17-18, NIV

I laugh when I see leaders doing everything within their power to discredit the past and those who came before them; it reeks of immaturity and sheer ignorance. We have modern leaders who, upon taking positions of authority, their first act of power is to almost erase the past. While I do agree that there are certain deeds that must be corrected, actions of such nature must be done with wisdom.

There are a few positive actions of the past that can be built upon for the public good. In the case of Isaac, he had become a very wealthy man through the blessings of God, and his wealth continued to grow until it attracted great envy from the Philistines. There were ancient wells opened by his father Abraham, and it is said that he reopened them and even gave them the same names his father had given them.

Godly leaders must understand the necessity of building on

past successes; not everything is going to be new and never been seen before. The test sometimes of your maturity is to be a conduit of continuity, which takes a level of self-confidence.

Dear leader, you can build on the past successes of others; it doesn't diminish you as a leader but amplifies your acumen in putting others first before yourself.

- ◈ 5 -

DISCERNMENT IN IDENTIFYING AND REWARDING TALENT

"Then Pharaoh said to Joseph, "Since God has made all this known to you, there is no one so discerning and wise as you. You shall be in charge of my palace, and all my people are to submit to your orders. Only with respect to the throne will I be greater than you."
—Genesis 41:39-40, NIV

"So, Pharaoh said to Joseph, "I hereby put you in charge of the whole land of Egypt." Then Pharaoh took his signet ring from his finger and put it on Joseph's finger. He dressed him in robes of fine linen and put a gold chain around his neck. He had him ride in a chariot as his second-in-command, and people shouted before him, "Make way!" Thus, he put him in charge of the whole land of Egypt. Then Pharaoh said to Joseph, "I am Pharaoh, but without your word no one will lift hand or foot in all Egypt."
—Genesis 41:41-44, NIV

The story of Joseph in the Bible is widely known, and he is the poster boy of the prison-to-palace tale retold over thousands of years, but the story of his epic rise also presents us with a leadership gem. Pharaoh displayed a key quality of discernment and reward in his encounter with the young Hebrew boy.

Joseph was nominated by a palace aide, who had been a beneficiary of his gift of interpretation when Pharaoh had two dreams that could not be interpreted even by the hordes of spiritualists and mediums in the royal court. For emphasis sake, it must be reinforced that the Egyptian Pharaohs were not your usual kings; the Egyptians viewed their rulers as the bridge between the realms of the spiritual and physical; he was a god in their eyes and commanded so much manpower and resources that would be mind-blowing to our modern minds.

Joseph would appear before Pharaoh announcing an impending disaster to sweep across the world, and the duality of the dreams was a confirmation of the inevitability of its occurrence. Pharaoh must have been wowed by the accuracy and confidence of the Hebrew slave, but even more importantly, he was discerning that he possessed something that others did not have and must be rewarded accordingly.

He specifically speaks to the wisdom and the presence of the spirit of God, good qualities that will further help to amplify his reign in a future that could destroy his empire. He would also reward Joseph greatly, primarily because of his ability to provide a three-pronged solution to shield Egypt from the famine by identifying systems, structures, and people who would make this Herculean task a reality. Pharaoh's act is a pointer to what any good leader should possess: a discerning spirit for talent and also a reward for their gifts. It is important in your leadership journey to reward subordinates that amplify your leadership position.

- 💎 6 -

INNOVATION

"And all the world came to Egypt to buy grain from Joseph, because the famine was severe everywhere."
—Genesis 41:57, NIV

"And now let Pharaoh look for a discerning and wise man and put him in charge of the land of Egypt. Let Pharaoh appoint commissioners over the land to take a fifth of the harvest of Egypt during the seven years of abundance. They should collect all the food of these good years that are coming and store up the grain under the authority of Pharaoh, to be kept in the cities for food. This food should be held in reserve for the country, to be used during the seven years of famine that will come upon Egypt, so that the country may not be ruined by the famine." The plan seemed good to Pharaoh and to all his officials."
—Genesis 41:33-37, NIV

"There was no food, however, in the whole region because the famine was severe; both Egypt and Canaan wasted away because of the famine. Joseph collected all the money that was to be found in Egypt and Canaan in payment for the grain they were buy-ing, and he brought it to Pharaoh's palace. When the money of the people of Egypt and Canaan was gone, all Egypt came to Joseph and said, "Give us food. Why should we die before your eyes? Our money is all gone." "Then bring your livestock," said Joseph. "I will sell you food in exchange for your livestock, since your money is gone." So, they brought their livestock

to Joseph, and he gave them food in exchange for their horses, their sheep and goats, their cattle and donkeys. And he brought them through that year with food in exchange for all their livestock. When that year was over, they came to him the following year and said, "We cannot hide from our Lord the fact that since our money is gone and our livestock belongs to you, there is nothing left for our Lord except our bodies and our land. Why should we perish before your eyes—we and our land as well? Buy us and our land in exchange for food, and we with our land will be in bondage to Pharaoh. Give us seed so that we may live and not die, and that the land may not become desolate." So, Joseph bought all the land in Egypt for Pharaoh. The Egyptians, one and all, sold their fields, because the famine was too severe for them. The land became Pharaoh's, and Joseph reduced the people to servitude, from one end of Egypt to the other. Joseph said to the people, "Now that I have bought you and your land today for Pharaoh, here is seed for you so you can plant the ground. But when the crop comes in, give a fifth of it to Pharaoh. The other four-fifths you may keep as seed for the fields and as food for yourselves and your households and your children." "You have saved our lives," they said. "May we find favor in the eyes of our Lord; we will be in bondage to Pharaoh." So, Joseph established it as a law concerning land in Egypt—still in force today—that a fifth of the produce belongs to Pharaoh. It was only the land of the priests that did not become Pharaoh's.
—Genesis 47:13-21, 23-26, NIV

Look at the world around you, and if you are sincere, you will see that God is the leading innovator in the universe; through His Spirit, He introduced new methods, ideas, etc. Godly leaders therefore must be innovators, and Joseph was no exception. He successfully combined what I have always advocated as the triad that runs success in any setting—the three key elements of people, systems, and structures—to guarantee the survival of the nation of Egypt. His suggestion for Pharaoh to find an overseer and appoint commissioners highlighted the importance of people to any leadership initiative.

Secondly, he instituted the construction of novel food reserves all across the country to house grain, which at the beginning was measured, but at a point was abandoned due to the vastness of produce collected (and which some countries around the world use till date to guarantee food security).

Lastly, he instituted systems of sales and trade by barter when money was no longer available. His innovation made Pharaoh a wealthy man in the season of the greatest famine on earth. His leadership saw that in a space of seven years, Pharaoh effectively owned the entire country due to unparalleled innovation.

In your leadership journey, what innovation are you introducing to your sphere of operation? Regardless of your standing on the ladder of leadership, you can always introduce innovation that will guarantee provisions and success despite the season.

Godly leaders must be strategic innovators to truly lead effectively in the 21st century and beyond. With daily global challenges, those being led seek leaders like you and me with the capacity to innovate.

- 💎 7 -

DON'T BARGAIN AWAY YOUR ORDAINED LEADERSHIP FOR A (FLEETING) MOMENT OF PLEASURE OR ANGER

"Reuben, you are my firstborn, my might, the first sign of my strength, excelling in honor, excelling in power. Turbulent as the waters, you will no longer excel, for you went up onto your father's bed, onto my couch and defiled it."
—Genesis 49:3-4, NIV

"Simeon and Levi are brothers— their swords are weapons of violence. Let me not enter their council, let me not join their assembly, for they have killed men in their anger and hamstrung oxen as they pleased. Cursed be their anger, so fierce, and their fury, so cruel! I will scatter them in Jacob and disperse them in Israel."
—Genesis 49:5-7, NIV

The Patriarchs passed across leadership to another generation by way of blessings and Jacob was no exception. He had twelve sons who would be the fathers of the twelve tribes of Israel. After living a very eventful life as is customary, his children gathered themselves to him for the blessing, and one very important element was that the messiah would come from one of the tribes, probably a fact that wasn't obvious.

Reuben no doubt must have felt important on this epoch-making event, to receive the blessing of leadership over his brothers, the stakes were very high because God's word to Abraham would not return to him but be accomplished. When he spoke, what Reuben received was a loss of his leadership as first son despite being praised as the first strength of a man. This happened because he slept with one of his father's concubines and received a curse of failure all his days (a curse that Moses would subsequently reverse). The next two brothers Simeon and Levi were not left off the hook; they had both displayed extreme violence, especially in the revenge of the defilement of their sister Dinah by Shechem and the death of all the men in the city, as well as innocent animals. On this account, they lost their leadership positions.

Judah had the leadership crown placed on him, receiving a treasure trove of blessings, the most important being the scepter never departing from that tribe and why today Jesus is called the Lion of the tribe of Judah.

Godly leaders must ensure that they do not allow vices rob them of leadership rights. This gem often ignored is one of the reasons why people get skipped when it comes to leadership selection. Jacob had all his life observed his sons and was in prime position to know who was deserving of leading the other tribes.

Walk in the consciousness that both God and men keep a keen eye on those suitable to lead others.

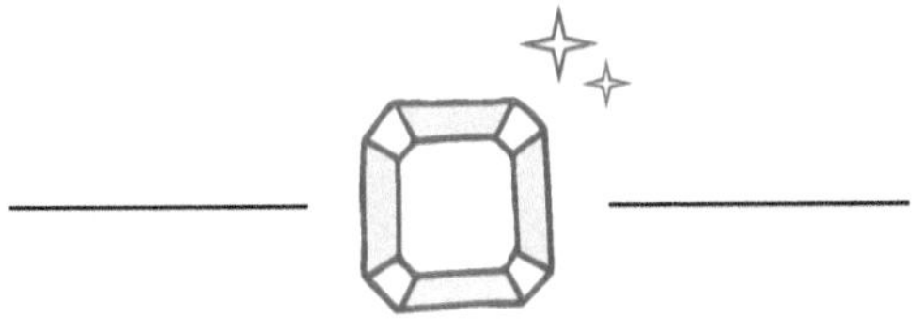

THE BOOK OF
EXODUS

- ◻8 -

PUBLIC SPEAKING & PERSUATION

"Then the Lord's anger burned against Moses, and he said, "What about your brother, Aaron the Levite? I know he can speak well. He is already on his way to meet you, and he will be glad to see you. You shall speak to him and put words in his mouth; I will help both of you speak and will teach you what to do. He will speak to the people for you, and it will be as if he were your mouth and as if you were God to him."
—Exodus 4:14-16, NIV

I am biased when it comes to public speaking and the resultant powerful effect of persuasion on listeners; maybe this is hinged on my past legal training and my present role as a public speaker to thousands globally. On a firsthand basis, I know the importance of a leader to confidently and eloquently marshall out their thoughts and convictions to get the necessary alignment.

Therefore, the exchange between Moses and the I AM THAT I AM was not really surprising; both parties knew a major necessity would be effective communication to convince Pharaoh to let the Israelites go on one hand and convince a nation of millions after a 400-year slavery season to follow a stammering fugitive into the desert to worship a God who at that point was unknown to the majority of them, save for oral tradition passed on from when Jacob and 69 ancestors made Goshen their home.

God's anger was directed at the litany of excuses Moses listed not to carry out his destiny, in one instance asking him who made the body parts. But God went ahead and got a communicator in Aaron, the elder brother of the chosen leader; Moses was to speak words, which would then be repeated when necessary to the elders and at the Royal Court of Ramses.

As a leader in today's modern world, you cannot jettison or wish away the importance of public speaking and its inherent ability to make men do what they ordinarily would not do due to the persuasive nature of the right words uttered by a competent leader. While I agree we may not all be like the great orators admired, it shouldn't limit the potential that exist when you put in the work to get better.

Finally, what is instructive to note is that after Exodus, no reference is given to the speech impairment of Moses, and up until his death, he spoke on numerous occasions to millions without the aid of Aaron.

Want to lead effectively? You must possess the gem of public speaking and persuasion.

- 09 -

A THICK SKIN

"The Israelite overseers realized they were in trouble when they were told, "You are not to reduce the number of bricks required of you for each day." When they left Pharaoh, they found Moses and Aaron waiting to meet them, and they said, "May the Lord look on you and judge you! You have made us obnoxious to Pharaoh and his officials and have put a sword in their hand to kill us."
—Exodus 5:19-21, NIV

Leadership requires a thick skin. By any stretch you want to consider it,you will most likely be faced with opposition from within and without, that could cause you to question yourself and what you represent.

Moses received a divine mandate to liberate the Hebrews from the shackles of their slave masters; he did everything right, followed God's instruction, and confronted Pharaoh who laughed in the face of what looked like a slave rebellion. He instructed that the quota of bricks to be produced remained in place, while straw would no longer be provided to the Israelite workers for the huge architectural masterpieces that the ancient Egyptians were known for. This caused deep resentment, leading to some representatives approaching the royal courts to plead for mercy. After being rebuffed by the god king, they went looking for the instigators, Moses and Aaron, and accused them to their faces of being responsible for inviting woe on the people who were already stretched beyond their limits. Moses turned to the lord, asking why he had become the face of trouble for his people and why he was the sent one. God assured him of His strong hand that will move against the Egyptian people to secure the freedom of Israel. Despite this heavenly assurance, the people did not listen because of their discouragement and labour. This was before the plagues came raining down.

All leaders, at one point in time or another, will face harsh criticism, untold disappointment, and unfair discouragement, but it is vital that you have a tough skin, since often times the opposition may be much closer than expected.

I sincerely believe God was preparing Moses to grow a thick skin to deal with the disappointment and pain both from his people and Pharaoh. God, in one word, could have ended what seemed to be the battle of the gods (with each plagued systematically making a mockery of an Egyptian pantheon of gods), but He allowed the confrontation to be drawn out for several reasons, and one was to strengthen the faith and character of the leader, Moses.

Are you aspiring to lead? You must be reminded that it will not always going to be a bed of roses; if you don't grow a tough skin, you may find yourself discouraged, frustrated, and throwing in the towel, something Moses attempted on several occasions. A gem to possess for all leaders is a thick skin for the opposition, whether it be scourging words or stinging actions. Be prepared; it will come.

- 💎 10 -

HOPE

"As Pharaoh approached, the Israelites looked up, and there were the Egyptians, marching after them. They were terrified and cried out to the Lord. They said to Moses, "Was it because there were no graves in Egypt that you brought us to the desert to die? What have you done to us by bringing us out of Egypt? Didn't we say to you in Egypt, 'Leave us alone; let us serve the Egyptians'? It would have been better for us to serve the Egyptians than to die in the desert!"
—Exodus 14:10-12, NIV

"Moses answered the people, "Do not be afraid. Stand firm and you will see the deliverance the Lord will bring you today. The Egyptians you see today you will never see again. The Lord will fight for you; you need only to be still." Then the Lord said to Moses, "Why are you crying out to me? Tell the Israelites to move on."
—Exodus 14:13-15, NIV

It has been said and quite accurately that a leader is a dealer in hope. Moses appeared from the desert to announce to the Israelites that God had remembered them and would lead them out of their 400-year captivity. After a barrage of plagues visited the Egyptians, the death of every firstborn (both human and animal) seemed to have broken the camel's back, with Pharaoh giving the Israelites their independence to go and worship God.

Unfortunately, the scales fell of the eyes of the Egyptians who assembled his best chariots and soldiers to overtake the former slaves; the only thing that separated the Israelites from their former task masters was the Red Sea. At that point all hope was lost, with Moses accused of leading them to death. At that point, after communing with God, the first thing he told the people was what anyone being led needs in tough times, hope.

Hope has within it the capacity to turn individuals from weaklings to strong beings, to turn fear into faith, and to inspire individuals to keep their eyes on the vision. If you are a leader, you must possess a steady supply of hope to dish out; sometimes, even if you are quaking in your boots, you must never stop dealing in hope.

- ◻11 -

TEAMWORK

"So, Joshua fought the Amalekites as Moses had ordered, and Moses, Aaron and Hur went to the top of the hill. As long as Moses held up his hands, the Israelites were winning, but whenever he lowered his hands, the Amalekites were winning. When Moses' hands grew tired, they took a stone and put it under him, and he sat on it. Aaron and Hur held his hands up—one on one side, one on the other—so that his hands remained steady till sunset. So, Joshua overcame the Amalekite army with the sword."
—*Exodus 17:10-13, NIV*

Teamwork is a prerequisite for any leader, and Moses recognized this jewel. The Amalekites were the inhabitants that confronted the young nation of Israel in their quest to take over the promised land flowing with milk and honey. The armies clashed in the valley, which would have been a bloody sight, but that particular battle was multidimensional in nature (spiritual and physical).

While Joshua led the Israelites as ordered by Moses, he climbed up a hill with Aaron, his brother, and Hur. It is recorded that for as long as they held up his hands, the Israelites won, and the tide turned when, out of fatigue, they let them down. This they did until Joshua overcame the enemy. The importance of a team is now on full display. Regardless of the encounters that accompanied his life,

Moses needed other men to work as a team to conquer the Amalekites.

To successfully lead, you must not jettison the importance of working with a team. Moses needed Joshua to fight and Aaron and Hur to hold him up. The question is, do you have such a team that will guarantee you victory in the battles of life?

- ◈ 12 -

DELEGATION

"The next day Moses took his seat to serve as judge for the people, and they stood around him from morning till evening. When his father-in-law saw all that Moses was doing for the people, he said, "What is this you are doing for the people? Why do you alone sit as judge, while all these people stand around you from morning till evening?" Moses answered him, "Because the people come to me to seek God's will. Whenever they have a dispute, it is brought to me, and I decide between the parties and inform them of God's decrees and instructions." Moses' father-in-law replied, "What you are doing is not good. You and these people who come to you will only wear yourselves out. The work is too heavy for you; you cannot handle it alone. Listen now to me, and I will give you some advice, and may God be with you. You must be the people's representative before God and bring their disputes to him. Teach them his decrees and instructions and show them the way they are to live and how they are to behave. But select capable men from all the people—men who fear God, trustworthy men who hate dishonest gain—and appoint them as officials over thousands, hundreds, fifties, and tens. Have them serve as judges for the people at all times, but have them bring every difficult case to you; the simple cases they can decide themselves. That will make your load lighter because they will share it with you. If you do this and God so commands, you will be able to stand the strain, and all these people will go home

satisfied." Moses listened to his father-in-law and did
everything he said."
—Exodus 18:13-24 NIV

We have often heard or used the term delegation at one point or another. This is simply the act of empowering to act for another. Delegation is another leadership gem highlighted in the book of Exodus. Moses led millions of Israelites on their way to the promised land, and you can expect the bickering and neighbourhood clashes amongst thousands. I live in a community of over two hundred homes, which I lead and know this firsthand—the mental drain in adjudicating issues.

Moses took his seat, and from morning to evening judged over matters, a physical endeavour that would leave for worse even the best of leaders. His father-in-law, Jethro, came visiting and noticed this anomaly in leadership. He critiqued the methodology being employed and told his son-in-law that the work was too heavy, and clearly Moses ran the risk of not finishing the race.

We can see that God permitted the intelligence of a man to employ a strategy around this. Jethro advised him to select capable men who feared God and were trustworthy and appoint them officials over select numbers (a semblance to our modern courts of jurisdiction). These men were to judge over simple cases to lighten the load, and the most difficult cases were reserved for Moses (a semblance to the Supreme Court). The result was a lighter load, and the people having justice dispensed quickly since justice delayed is justice denied and could lead to a breakdown of law and order. By having justice, a leader brings stability. Every leader must employ delegation in the same manner; it is an impossibility to apply yourself to every situation and decision-making; rather, wisdom dictates you delegate to others, who can carry a chunk of your workload, giving you the clarity and peace to deal with the most important decisions that land on your table.

- 13 -

LEADERSHIP IN YOUR ABSENCE

*"Then Moses set out with Joshua his aide, and Moses
went up on the mountain of God. He said to the elders, "Wait here for us until we come back to you.
Aaron and Hur are with you, and anyone involved in
a dispute can go to them."*
—Exodus 24:13-14, NIV

The Lord ordered Moses to approach him on the mountain,
stay there, and receive the tablets of stone containing the law
and commandments he had written for their instruction.
Now this was a young nation of a few millions of former
slaves who had been in servitude. Like any wise leader,
Moses understood that a leadership lapse in his absence
could not be tolerated, so he took the necessary steps to
ensure that governance continued uninterrupted.

Moses addressed the seventy elders of Israel, who
ascended and encountered Israel's God. He told them he
had appointed Aaron and Hur to handle all disputes in
his absence. Many leaders can afford to go on vacations
or other engagements, caring less about what will happen
in their absence; they create an environment where the
people cannot rely on leadership at all times, whether it is
intentional or not.

Moses is teaching godly leaders the principle of replacement:

never be so important that you fill a position, that no one is good bought to take your role in your absence. I personally run with a mental philosophy that everyone is dispensable, not to belittle their gifting and talents but understanding that the visccitudes of life can change the equation and life will go on.

A true leader must never leave a vacuum.

- ⬡ 14 -

STANDING IN THE GAP

"Now leave me alone so that my anger may burn against them and that I may destroy them. Then I will make you into a great nation." But Moses sought the favor of the Lord his God. "Lord," he said, "why should your anger burn against your people, whom you brought out of Egypt with great power and a mighty hand? Why should the Egyptians say, 'It was with evil intent that he brought them out, to kill them in the mountains and to wipe them off the face of the earth'? Turn from your fierce anger; relent and do not bring disaster on your people. Remember your servants Abraham, Isaac and Israel, to whom you swore by your own self: 'I will make your descendants as numerous as the stars in the sky and I will give your descendants all this land I promised them, and it will be their inheritance forever. Then the Lord relented and did not bring on his people the disaster he had threatened."
—Exodus 32:10-14, NIV

If I were permitted to personally describe what I think should be at the heart of every leader, it would be sacrifice, and that, in my opinion, is one of the greatest expressions of Moses's leadership acumen. The children of Israel had done the unthinkable (at least by human standards, as nothing escapes the all-knowing God).

God had called Moses up the Sinai mountain to receive the

marriage contract between both parties; he had been gone for about a month when the people forgot all their eyes had witnessed and gave in to the debauchery of their flesh, causing God to immediately inform their leader to depart from him so he could visit them with his vengeance and destroy them. In a swift moment, he offered Moses a once in a lifetime opportunity to plead for an entire nation born from his loins, proposing to change the entire trajectory of the promises made to the patriarchs (Abraham, Isaac, and Jacob). I often wonder how many people would turn down such a once in the earth opportunity, but that's exactly what Moses did; he immediately stepped into the gap, standing between the vengeance of a just and holy God and a people who were unable to keep their promises.

It would be so easy for a leader to have his people thrown under the bus after all it was not his doing, but instead Moses soaked in the intensity of the anger emanating from the presence of the ageless creator of the universe, lying prostrate for forty days and forty nights, and afterward the Lord relented and did not bring on His people the disaster He had threatened. A leader per excellence is anyone who takes this gem; he would have his name written with the stars and constellations for all days.

- ◻ 15 -

NEVER LOSE CONTROL OR SIGHT OF THE BIGGER PICTURE

"Moses saw that the people were running wild, and that Aaron had let them get out of control and so become a laughingstock to their enemies."
—*Exodus 32:25, NIV*

To continue with our last gem, Moses had just descended from the mountain with his trusted aide Joshua, carrying two large stones on which God Himself had inscribed the Ten Commandments for the Israelites. Initially, Joshua mistakenly believed that their enemies might be attacking the camp, but Moses clarified that the noise and ruckus was that of celebration.

Upon descent, he saw the people running wild and, to make matters worse, had built themselves a golden calf made from the very gold they had received from the Egyptians according to God's promise, giving it worship for their deliverance. The sight would have been too overwhelming even for the meekest man on earth, but what was instructive was the failure of one leader who lost control and vision of the bigger picture.

The nation of Israel was under the care of Aaron, who should have known better having occupied a front row seat from the moment of the burning bush to the wilderness, but it is recorded he let them get out of control, making them a laughingstock to their enemies.

A leader must never let those being led lose control; it is a major failure and a question on the capabilities of such an individual. Secondly, he lost sight of the bigger picture of what God had told him and his brother Moses, and as a result, the fear of the people made him drop the ball of leadership. At all times, a leader must have a face set like a flint on the bigger picture.

- 16 -

ENFORCE DISCIPLINE

"So, he stood at the entrance to the camp and said, "Whoever is for the Lord, come to me." And all the Levites rallied to him. Then he said to them, "This is what the Lord, the God of Israel, says: Each man strap a sword to his side. Go back and forth through the camp from one end to the other, each killing his brother and friend and neighbor."
—Exodus 32:26-27, NIV

Personal experience has shown that disciplining subordinates is one of the hardest tasks. It's often difficult to decide what specific action to take, but Moses stood out as a leader. Upon taking over the reins of authority from Aaron, his very first act back in his leadership capacity was to enforce discipline by punishing those who had brought such evil into the midst of God's people. Standing at the camp entrance, he declared the presence of loyal elements among the people, prompting the Levites to rally behind him.

Aaron's leadership failure led to a massacre of brothers, friends, and neighbours, resulting in the deaths of three thousand people. While we cannot replicate such harsh measures in contemporary times, it is important to note that a wise leader understands that if they fail to address a failure among their followers, it will eventually spread and become a cancer, ultimately leading to a system shutdown.

The gem, therefore, is to be a strict leader who must never be afraid to take the necessary steps to enforce discipline, even when it's difficult to execute; a failure on this may have far more dangerous repercussions for your position and legacy.

- ◻ 17 -

RESPONSIBILITY

"But now, please forgive their sin—but if not, then blot me out of the book you have written."
—Exodus 32:32, NIV

It takes a lot of leadership molecules in the body of an individual to take responsibility and be ready to pay the ultimate price for those you lead, and this very well may have been why Moses was clearly special in the eyes of God. I often think that at this juncture, he foreshadowed what Jesus Christ would do a few thousand years later by taking the place of all humanity to carry the sins of the world. Moses touched God's heart by asking for the forgiveness of the sins of those he was leading, and he was prepared to sacrifice his eternity in exchange. Such selflessness is not only rare but nearly impossible to find in those ancient times, let alone in our current era.

A leader must take full responsibility and bear the full weight of the punishment he did not deserve. His encounters made him clearly aware that God had written a book about humanity, and he was willing to erase himself from its pages due to the actions of a few thousand renegades who had betrayed God by pursuing their selfish desires. A leader must have a spirit of responsibility. I once heard a story in my country about a late Bank Chief Executive who, upon his passing, was said to have physically prostrated in front of the financial regulator for a financial punishment to be meted out to his bank. This was not because he did anything wrong or because it could be paid, but because he understood that leadership comes with responsibility. Often, this responsibility extends to the actions of those you lead. Moses understood this principle and likely postponed what could have been a swift judgment to a subtler one, as evidenced by scripture.

- 18 -

THE PRESENCE

"Moses said to the Lord, "You have been telling me, 'Lead these people,' but you have not let me know whom you will send with me. You have said, 'I know you by name and you have found favor with me.' The Lord replied, "My Presence will go with you, and I will give you rest."
—Exodus 33:12-14, NIV

"Lord," he said, "if I have found favor in your eyes, then let the Lord go with us. Although this is a stiff-necked people, forgive our wickedness and our sin, and take us as your inheritance."
—Exodus 34:9, NIV

The presence of God in a godly leader is what distinguishes such an exceptional leader or individual, and Moses understood this clearly. He was leading a nation of a few million individuals, many of whom had never known freedom and were evidently mentally imprisoned. It was a Herculean task, and despite his training in the school of the wilderness at the household of his father-in-law, Jethro, he knew he faced an almost insurmountable obstacle to go through the harsh desert and overtake a territory that was already occupied.

It is for this reason that he knew the presence of God would be the deciding factor between success and failure.

Moses demonstrated a pattern for leaders, recognizing that navigating a journey filled with immense uncertainty necessitates a higher level of intelligence. This is why he prayed for God's presence to accompany him, a request that God granted, resulting in his leadership becoming more effective. First, the presence brought him rest; secondly, it manifested itself in the form of cloud and fire elements, which God used to guide them through various times and seasons. His presence also ensured sustenance, as they lacked the means to produce food for millions.

Therefore, as a leader, it is crucial to recognize that having the presence of the one who is always present is a valuable asset.

- ◻ 19 -

FAVOURITISM

"Don't pass on malicious gossip. "Don't link up with a wicked person and give corrupt testimony. Don't go along with the crowd in doing evil and don't mess up your testimony in a case just to please the crowd. And just because someone is poor, don't show favoritism in a dispute."
—Exodus 23:1-3, MSG

"And do not show favoritism to a poor person in a lawsuit."
—Exodus 23:3, NIV

One of the banana peels that litter the hallway of leadership must be that of favouritism. Once an individual commands influence, there is every temptation for your decisions to sway towards the benefits of a certain class of people. Now, while there is nothing wrong with showing favouritism in itself, what is important is that it should be directed towards those who are deserving of such favour.

God was telling Moses the risk that runs amok when a certain person is shown favouritism not because they are right or wrong, but primarily because of their social standing and possessions. In modern leadership, the charismatic nature of leaders can attract a diverse range of individuals, and their possession of authority can lead to a tendency to show favouritism during disputes. God wants leaders to be fair in all dealings.

- ◻ 20 -

FAIRNESS

"Do not deny justice to your poor people in their lawsuits."
—Exodus 23:6, NIV

It's often easy to find individuals who would profess that every bone in their bodies is made up of fairness, until they are called or appointed to lead. People in our modern world often hold the belief that laws favour the rich over the poor, but the truth is, this wickedness predates the creation of our current legal systems.

Moses understood that fairness is one of the characteristics of what the late speaker Myles Monroe described as the Spirit of Leadership. One of the most frequent tasks you will be called upon to do is adjudicate between individuals, and Moses is advocating that we should never let the size of a person's bank account influence our judgement.

Whenever you sit in a position of authority, it should be a sacred duty to uphold fairness in all dealings. Everyone, even if they are not equal on the social ladder, should never be less equal in the eyes of a true leader. A fair leader is one who will always make strides and have the people on his side at all times and the blessings of God. So, as you go on leading, lead with the gem of fairness; history is always kind to fair rulers.

- 21 -

BRIBERY

*"Do not accept a bribe, for a bribe blind those who
see and twists the words of the innocent."*
—*Exodus 23:8, NIV*

We have a pandemic of corruption wreaking havoc on nations, organizations, education, and, most unfortunately, the church, which should be at the forefront of righteous living. It is almost never a surprise when a leader has been found to receive a bribe to influence things to go the way of someone or something, almost like it is now the second nature to leaders closer to them than their own skin.

Moses warned the leaders of Israel to repel all bribes, giving the negative effect when even a single dose is swallowed. Bribe blinds the eyes of the receiver and twists the words of such a person. Sometimes, if you find a leader oblivious to some harsh truth or reality of something negative, it may be evidence that they have been compromised. Bribe zips up the mouths of leaders and steals their voice in the process.

This gem is so important because nothing has rubbished most leaders more than the scourge of bribe taking; a simple online search will buttress this point. You want to be effective with eyes that see everything and a functional mouth to speak and act as a leader; do not accept a bribe. Flee!

- ◻ 22 -

OPPRESSION

"Do not oppress a foreigner; you yourselves know how it feels to be foreigners, because you were foreigners in Egypt."
—Exodus 23:9, NIV

Unfortunately, oppression is now commonplace, especially towards those who don't look or even sound like us; it's widespread across many nations of the earth, and ancient Israel was no exception. During the exodus from Egypt, it is on record that some Israelites and those of other nationalities, I presume after seeing the majestic hand of the Lord visiting vengeance on Pharaoh, elected to follow this Hebrew God. Also in the promised lands there were also eventually going to have foreigners in their midst.

It is for this reason that Moses advocated that oppression of foreigners be far from the Israelites, because they were once foreigners and tasted the bitterness of their oppressors, with many still carrying scars from the whips of the task masters. Leaders, wherever they are found in any sphere of influence, must show kindness to all men regardless of their origin or background. leaders must advocate that their people are fair and kind, never showing hostility and pain to other men. You want to lead well and kick out oppression in any form, whether against your own followers or those who are not related to you.

- ◻ 23 -

STRATEGIC GROWTH AND EXPANSION

"I will send the hornet ahead of you to drive the Hivites, Canaanites and Hittites out of your way. But I will not drive them out in a single year, because the land would become desolate and the wild animals too numerous for you. Little by little I will drive them out before you, until you have increased enough to take possession of the land."
—Exodus 23:28-30, NIV

One of the key indicators of effective leadership is often growth and expansion. With this insight, we can draw conclusions from the unparalleled wisdom of God about the most effective ways to grow and expand. God had promised the Israelites the Fertile Crescent of Canaan, a land of milk and honey, where they would inherit centuries of hard work from those who had previously occupied the land.

From a leadership perspective, the move I may have made was to go in, guns blazing, taking over the inheritance promised by the God of my ancestors, but it was the very same God who promised the land that showed that growth and expansion must be strategic in nature. Often, as a business leader, I have made many mistakes not adopting this gem due to my haste and shortsightedness, or maybe just the sheer excitement, which I believe many of those following Moses must have felt.

However, there is always a strategy for growth and expansion, and your job as a leader is to find the right key for the right door, as no two scenarios are the same in nature. Moses was informed that God would employ a multipronged strategy to rid the land off its occupiers; he would send the hornet, a large swarm capable of driving men, cattle, and horses to madness due to their fierce and voracious nature. This action would not be completed in a single year to prevent the land from becoming desolate and overrun by wild beasts, but would instead be carried out systematically in phases.

I believe this gem contains within it abundant wisdom for leaders to adopt, especially when it comes to leaving their comfort zone into the unknown and being strategic when it comes to growth and expansion.

- ◻ 24 -

LEADERSHIP IN YOUR ABSENCE

"Then Moses set out with Joshua his aide, and Moses went up on the mountain of God. He said to the elders, "Wait here for us until we come back to you. Aaron and Hur are with you, and anyone involved in a dispute can go to them."
—Exodus 24:13-14, NIV

In any setting, the presence of a leader makes a significant difference, and the complete absence of a responsible figure is a recipe for trouble. Leaders must never encourage a vacuum, as even nature itself is known to resent it. Moses was called up by God to climb up the holy mountain, understanding that such an absence could lead to disaster. He expressly and publicly told the people that his brothers Aaron and Hur would be responsible for stepping into their shoes to settle any disputes that may well arise.

Many leaders take this gem almost with a pinch of salt and wonder why they come back to their homes, communities, organizations, and, in some extreme instances, countries (leaders have been known to leave the seat of power without transmitting the same to their deputies) in utter confusion. Scripture expounds on the wisdom displayed by Moses and which must be adopted by godly leaders who hold responsibilities to always make adequate preparation in selecting those who will hold forte in their absence to discourage a complete breakdown of law and order.

Have you ever seen a herd of animals without a shepherd? They don't follow the wisest or even the strongest; instead, each animal follows the one in front of them, and the first animal may not follow anyone at all. A leader in the making must always be present to lead when the main leader is unavoidably absent. This is a gem treasured by all godly leaders who understand they must never leave those who follow without the authority of an individual that embodies their vision.

- ◻ 25 -

LEADERSHIP IN YOUR ABSENCE

"All the Israelite men and women who were willing brought to the Lord freewill offerings for all the work the Lord through Moses had commanded them to do."
—Exodus 35:29, NIV

"These are the amounts of the materials used for the tabernacle, the tabernacle of the covenant law, which were recorded at Moses' command by the Levites under the direction of Ithamar son of Aaron, the priest."
—Exodus 38:21, NIV

One of the definitions of leadership that most excites me is the management of individuals and resources to reach a common goal, which mirrors exactly what Moses exhibited on a number of critical occasions. God issued a commandment, and Moses instructed the entire Israelite community to bring an offering.

The command was for everyone who was willing to bring an offering of gold, silver, and bronze, yarn and linen, wood, spices, oil, and precious stones for the construction of the tabernacle. The abundance of generosity prompted Moses to issue an order, disseminating throughout the camp the message that no individual should contribute, as their existing resources were sufficient to complete all the tasks. Moses will show himself as an efficient manager of resources when the amounts of the materials used were recorded at his command by the Levites under the direction of Ithamar, son of Aaron, the priest. The Levites audited and recorded the use of the gold, silver, and bronze they acquired from the community.

Regardless of their scope of operation, every leader must prioritize accountability; nothing fosters trust more effectively than this. When the people you lead have confidence in your resource management, your leadership exponentially grows. Leaders fall at this hurdle because of a nonchalant demeanour or a lack of attention to details, believing that it offers no significance. Moses inspected the work and saw that they had done it just as the Lord had commanded. Your creed in managing both men and resources should be nothing missing and nothing broken; a good leader suffers no loss on both the accounts of men and resources.

- 💎 26 -

MOVEMENT

"In all the travels of the Israelites, whenever the cloud lifted from above the tabernacle, they would set out; but if the cloud did not lift, they did not set out—until the day it lifted. So, the cloud of the Lord was over the tabernacle by day, and fire was in the cloud by night, in the sight of all the Israelites during all their travels."
—Exodus 40:36-38, NIV

We can compare a leader to a compass, a timeless navigation tool that has guided travellers for different millennia. A leader's primary responsibility is to guide his followers from their current location to their intended destination, a task that often presents its own set of challenges. Moses articulated that a leader must transcend his own capabilities to effectively guide those under his guidance, and the ultimate guidance can only originate from above.

The Children of Israel were faced with possible thousands of kilometres of nothing, a challenge to make sense of direction and enough to mess with your mental capabilities. The ageless wisdom of God that was present at the time of creation afforded Moses a navigational aide to help him lead the millions of freed slaves, in the form of a cloud. The cold nights in the desert would have been another tale, and God gave fire, which I believe gave navigation for nighttime travel and warmth as well.

Godly leaders don't move only with their wisdom but rely on spiritual intelligence when making decisions of movement. Moses understanding this gem may have necessitated his passionate prayer of the presence of God to help make the difficult movement easier. If you are a leader seeking to reach your promised land, lean not only on your own understanding when making movement.

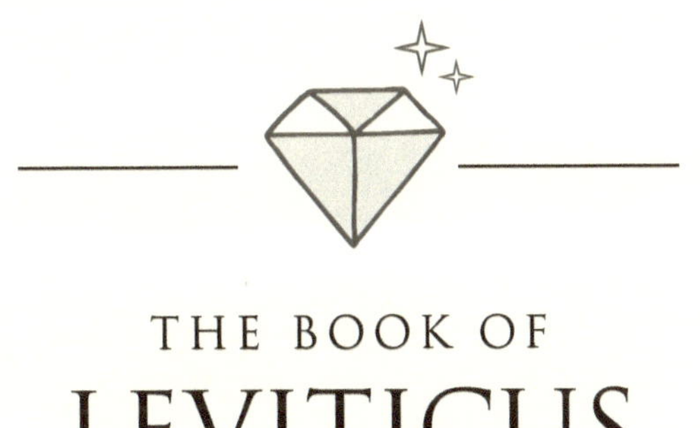

THE BOOK OF
LEVITICUS

- ◈ 27 -

ADHERENCE TO INSTRUCTIONS AND REGULATIONS

"Aaron's sons Nadab and Abihu took their censers, put fire in them and added incense; and they offered unauthorized fire before the Lord, contrary to his command. So fire came out from the presence of the Lord and consumed them, and they died before the Lord."
—Leviticus 10:1-2, NIV

It almost seems to be an unwritten rule of leadership, that is, rules are made for others and not for leaders. Many leaders are not humble enough to subject themselves to following laid-down rules and regulations. In many places you find leaders bending rules, unable to wait for stop lights, skip queues—the list is endless in nature, but what makes rules potent is that they should be applied and applicable to all regardless of status.

Societies that respect the rule of law are known to be more prosperous in nature. God had set up a long list of instructions for Aaron, the chosen priest of Israel, and his sons, who were all consecrated to him. The holiness of God demanded that certain rituals be observed as the physical environment had to mirror the heavens of heavens where He dwells, so I definitely did not envy the levites in their ordained role to God and his people.

Two of Aaron's sons, Nadab and Abihu, were two leaders who became victims of violating the respect that all leaders must have for instructions and regulations. They had been expressly warned about offering unauthorized fire before the Lord; unfortunately, they took their censers, put fire in them, and added incense contrary to the command, and the judgement was instant death as fire came out from the presence of the Lord and consumed them. They died before the Lord.

Their crime was simply not adhering to the laid-down protocol of those who had access to the presence of the God of all flesh. This unfortunate scenario provides leaders a timely lesson on how to follow regulations. Rules are meant to be obeyed even by those occupying lofty offices, while the punishment for disobeying may not be fire consuming you. The disgrace meted out to leaders who consider themselves to be above rules is never truly palatable.

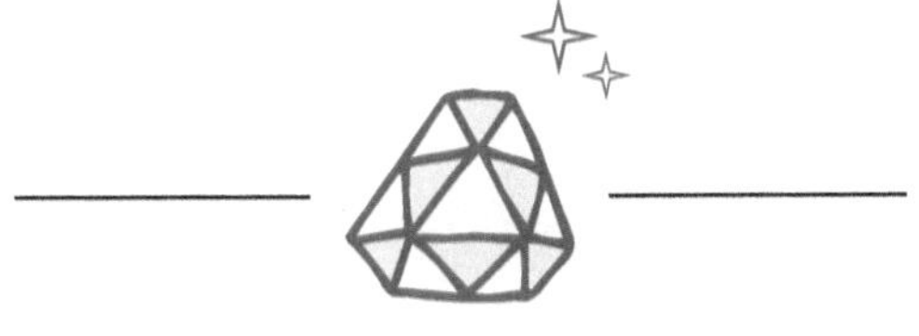

THE BOOK OF
NUMBERS

- ◈ 28 -

HUMILITY

"Now Moses was a very humble man, more humble than anyone else on the face of the earth."
—*Numbers 12:3, NIV*

There are various definitions of humility, but I particularly like the one offered by the Cambridge dictionary which is the feeling or attitude that you have no special importance that makes you better than others. You must understand that if there's any quality that must feature prominently in the ingredient mix of any leader, it is humility. The Scripture zeroes in expressly on the humility component of Moses, which most have rated highly in the leadership index of what God was looking for in a man who would be responsible in birthing a new nation (whose citizenry would be a stiff-necked people), and he needed a meek and very patient leader.

One can capture the weight of this godly acknowledgement when you take into cognizance the millions, if not billions, of humans on earth at the time. When reading the adventures through the wilderness, one can see how humility played a vital role in the leadership offered by Moses to the people. This humility often led God to fight for and defend Moses, a crucial lesson for any godly leader: always let humility lead the way.

God is never too far behind a humble man; he resists the proud and extends grace to the humble. If a man chooses a godly pathway to lead others, he must recognize the importance of imbibing within him a humble heart, one that puts others first, even sometimes at the expense of his own comfort. Godly leaders put a wide gulf between themselves and pride; they embrace humility on the other hand until they become one with it. Be Humble.

- 💠 29 -

COMMUNICATION METHODOLOGY

"Make two trumpets of hammered silver, and use them for calling the community together and for having the camps set out. When both are sounded, the whole community is to assemble before you at the entrance to the tent of meeting. If only one is sounded, the leaders—the heads of the clans of Israel—are to assemble before you. When a trumpet blast is sounded, the tribes camping on the east are to set out. At the sounding of a second blast, the camps on the south are to set out. The blast will be the signal for setting out. To gather the assembly, blow the trumpets, but not with the signal for setting out."
—Numbers 10:2-7 NIV

I absolutely love how God is detailed in everything, including communication methods. You can almost picture the scenario in an era of no communication, in a huge camp of millions of migrants, moving across vast areas of land, no phones, no emails. Absolutely nothing, maybe at best a runner to the tents of individuals Moses needed to communicate with; imagine also how long it would take to send word across the camp for a meeting or the movement when the cloud had lifted. Moses received instructions to craft two trumpets from hammered silver, which he would use for summoning the community and for departure.

Upon the sounding of both trumpets, the community

gathered at the meeting tent, with only one trumpet designated for leaders and for movement coordination. At other times, the trumpets served as a clarion call for battle against the oppressors. Modern leaders need to develop a strategy for communicating with their followers; they can't use the same approach for the entire organization. Your people must understand your communication methodology to ensure everyone remains on the same page. Many leaders fail not because they are poor at people or resource management, but chiefly because of their inability to have a clear communication methodology.

- ◈ 30 -

EXPERIENCED HELPERS

"Now Moses said to Hobab son of Reuel the Midianite, Moses' father-in-law, "We are setting out for the place about which the Lord said, 'I will give it to you.' Come with us and we will treat you well, for the Lord has promised good things to Israel." He answered, "No, I will not go; I am going back to my own land and my own people." But Moses said, "Please do not leave us. You know where we should camp in the wilderness, and you can be our eyes. If you come with us, we will share with you whatever good things the Lord gives us."
—Numbers 10:29-32, NIV

There is a common misconception that leaders are self-sufficient and do not require assistance, but a closer examination of Moses's leadership style reveals another valuable trait that every leader should strive to cultivate. Jethro (other times referred to as Reuel) was Moses' father-in-law, while Hobab was his son. It is evident from their exchange that Moses wanted to ride on the experience of his brother-in-law. You need to remember that these were nomads who knew the ways of the vast and dreadful desert, an often unforgiving stretch of sand dunes, filled with venomous snakes and scorpions, no vegetation, and scorching heat.

The cloud of the Lord had lifted from above the tabernacle, and the Israelites, tribe by tribe, under their standard, set out from Sinai until the cloud rested in the Desert of Paran. Moses instructed Hobab to accompany the Israelites to the promised land, promising a great reward in return. Whilst you may be forgiven to believe that this may have been a usual exchange between two relations, the motive would be identified. Moses was quick to appeal to him saying, "please do not leave us". You know where we should camp in the wilderness, and you can be our eyes and a promise of the good things God would give."

You can see that as a leader, Moses understood he was in unfamiliar terrain and needed someone with the requisite skill and knowledge of the desert; he needed Hobab to identify camp sites and also explore his experienced wilderness-trained eyes for the benefit of the countless thousands of Israel. As a leader, you need a Hobab, an experienced helper on your side who can help cover your blind side at all times.

- ✦ 31 -

LEADERSHIP DUPLICATION

"The Lord said to Moses: "Bring me seventy of Israel's elders who are known to you as leaders and officials among the people. Have them come to the tent of meeting, that they may stand there with you. I will come down and speak with you there, and I will take some of the power of the Spirit that is on you and put it on them. They will share the burden of the people with you so that you will not have to carry it alone."
— Numbers 11:16, 17, NIV

Moses was clearly at breaking point, like most leaders will be at some point in their leadership journey, nostalgic at the past, confused at the present and worried about the future. The children of Israel had started their complaints like many who are led and were touched by the fire from the Lord until Moses interceded. Yet the rabble continued about the food choice. God had given them manna (bread from heaven) on a daily basis, but instead they craved for meat to eat, dreaming about tasty fish from the Nile, cucumbers, and other vegetables. Their leader heard the people of every family complaining. He questioned why he was burdened with such a heavy burden, even pleading for death as a permanent solution.

However, God's wisdom revealed another valuable lesson

for leaders, emphasizing the difficulty of relying solely on oneself and the importance of delegating to others in order to effectively lead. The Lord asked Moses to bring him seventy elders who are known to him as leaders and officials, and he would descend and take some of the power of the spirit on Moses and put it on them so they could share the burden of the people so he wouldn't have to carry it alone.

A leader must passionately seek out duplicating himself in others to be truly successful; such individuals who should share your spirit are not there to amplify your personality but rather feel your pain and bear your burden to avoid you fizzling out. Smart leaders duplicate themselves across board; you cannot carry all the responsibilities depending on the scope of your position alone.

- ◈ 32 -

FEAR OF POSITION

> *"However, two men, whose names were Eldad and Medad, had remained in the camp. They were listed among the elders, but did not go out to the tent. Yet the Spirit also rested on them, and they prophesied in the camp. A young man ran and told Moses, "Eldad and Medad are prophesying in the camp." Joshua son of Nun, who had been Moses' aide since youth, spoke up and said, "Moses, my Lord, stop them!" But Moses replied, "Are you jealous for my sake? I wish that all the Lord's people were prophets and that the Lord would put his Spirit on them!"*
> —*Numbers 11:26-29 NIV*

There is one important element that is never fully admitted by most leaders, and that most be the fear of being outshined by others; this can be manifested through jealousy. It is often something hidden in the trenches and never really comes to the fore until heat makes it rear its head, like a serpent close to a fire. This fear is often the undoing of many leaders who become psychotic and view everyone else as a threat.

After the spirit of God came upon the elders selected to carry the burden with Moses, two elders, Eldad and Medad, were not present in the tent but in the camp. The spirit of God fell on them, and they started to prophesy. A young lad ran and told Moses, with Joshua his aide immediately asking Moses that they should be stopped. Moses would reply in a wise manner and drop the next leadership gem by declaring, "Are you jealous for my sake?" and like the confident leader that he was, he declared that his wish was that not just the seventy elders, but all of the Lord's people were prophets, and the Lord would put his spirit on them (Several centuries later, this would be a reality with God pouring out his spirit on all flesh, not just on leaders but all can receive).

It is acidic for a leader to harbour the thought of jealousy towards others who have similar gifting and manifestation; true leaders want to see all that they lead grow.

- ◈ 33 -

DEALING WITH DOMESTIC OPPOSITION

"Miriam and Aaron began to talk against Moses because of his Cushite wife, for he had married a Cushite. "Has the Lord spoken only through Moses?" they asked. "Hasn't he also spoken through us?" And the Lord heard this."
—Numbers 12:1, 2, NIV

It's one thing to have opposition from those outside your fold; you can imagine how difficult it will be for a leader when the problem starts to brew from within your household. Despite the miracles, wonders, and punishment, Miriam and Aaron would oppose their brother because of the choice of a spouse, asking if the Lord speaks only through Moses. This must have been very disheartening and difficult to bear, but I reckon that the scripture in Numbers 12:3 reminds us again of the humility of Moses buttresses my assumption that he let them be. It's one thing to declare punishment on others but a totally different kettle of fish when it's your own siblings (Miriam helped in saving Moses as an infant).

Godly leaders in such an unwelcome position realize they are caught between a rock and a hard place, and the wisdom gem was to allow God to do the recompensing. It was God who summoned a family meeting to express His displeasure and meted out the punishment to Mariam, who appeared to have been the chief instigator (bad sister-in-law), and she was cast out of the camp for a season.

Often times, as a leader, you can't fight all the battles, especially those at the home front. My advice is to follow the wisdom of letting God do what He will. The Bible says in Matthew 10:36 that a man's enemies will be the members of his own household. Such foes, whether justifiably right or wrong, can be an impediment for a godly leader. To explore this, the Holy Spirit must be relied upon to be able to marshal the requisite knowledge and wisdom required to stay above the drama.

- ◈ 34 -

AUDACITY

" But the people who live there are powerful, and the cities are fortified and very large. We even saw descendants of Anak there. The Amalekites live in the Negev; the Hittites, Jebusites and Amorites live in the hill country; and the Canaanites live near the sea and along the Jordan." Then Caleb silenced the people before Moses and said, "We should go up and take possession of the land, for we can certainly do it."
—Numbers 13:28-30, NIV

" Joshua son of Nun and Caleb son of Jephunneh, who were among those who had explored the land, tore their clothes and said to the entire Israelite assembly, "The land we passed through and explored is exceedingly good. If the Lord is pleased with us, he will lead us into that land, a land flowing with milk and honey, and will give it to us. Only do not rebel against the Lord. And do not be afraid of the people of the land, because we will devour them. Their protection is gone, but the Lord is with us. Do not be afraid of them."
—Numbers 14:6-9, NIV

The final verdict was out, and the stones were about to start flying from all different directions of the Israelite assembly towards the direction of Israelite leaders Moses and Aaron, who stood in front of the people. But first, a little backtrack on how we got here. The Lord had commanded

Prophet Moses to send men to explore the land of Canaan; from each of the twelve tribes a leader, they were on an espionage mission, a clandestine operation to sample the land that would be theirs. They beheld the fertility of the land, plucking grape clusters for consumption, admiring the animals and the beauty that lay before them, but one thing stood out: they encountered men who were giants and carried a bad report that ran counter to God's promise, spreading it among the people, saying the promised land will be their gravesites.

But two leaders shone brightly in a dark moment; they possessed audacity. The first leader to exhibit the gem of audacity was Caleb from Judah (a little surprise about the tribe). He silenced the people, declaring that they go up and take possession of the land, for we can certainly do it. This did little to soften the aggression as the community raised their voices and wept; even suggestions were made to choose a new leader and return to Egypt. It was at this point that the second leader, Joshua, would show courage, advising the riotous mob not to sin again against God but instead discard fear and take on the land and its inhabitants. It was at this point God elected again to destroy the nation with a plague (a second time) offering to make Moses into a nation (and for the second time he declined instead interceding); this will lead to the punishment that none of the Israelites who saw his glory will see the promised land (and a long sojourn of forty years began). The only exception were the two brave, audacious leaders Joshua and Caleb, who got their reward. A leader must be ready to face opposition and have the audacity to carry through his faith convictions; there are great rewards that await such an individual.

- ◈ 35 -

LEGITIMACY OF AUTHORITY

"Speak to the Israelites and get twelve staffs from them, one from the leader of each of their ancestral tribes. Write the name of each man on his staff. On the staff of Levi write Aaron's name, for there must be one staff for the head of each ancestral tribe. Place them in the tent of meeting in front of the ark of the covenant law, where I meet with you. The staff belonging to the man I choose will sprout, and I will rid myself of this constant grumbling against you by the Israelites." The next day Moses entered the tent and saw that Aaron's staff, which represented the tribe of Levi, had not only sprouted but had budded, blossomed and produced almonds."
—*Numbers 17:2-5, 8, NIV*

Leadership is always going to be challenged; it comes with the position, and to put an end to ceaseless grumbling, it is important that there is a sign to the rebellious. Every leadership must have a flow from where it derives its authority and, invariably, its legitimacy to act. God was tired of the incessant grumbling the leadership of Moses and Aaron as priests was attracting; at every turn there seemed to be individuals challenging his right to lead.

Leading to the above verse was the insolence of Koran, Dathan, and Abram, along with 250 others who challenged Moses and Aaron, with Moses declaring they went too far. Both parties appeared before God with incense to select who was chosen. What happened next was a horror movie, leading to the earth swallowing alive the rebels, their families, and belongings, and the other 250 being incinerated by Holy Fire. After this gory episode, the very next day, another rebellion reared its head, leading to the death of 14,700 people from a plague.

God decided to get each tribe leader to drop their staff, which was the symbol of authority, in front of the tent of the covenant, and the man chosen his staff will sprout. The next day, Moses entered the tent and saw that Aaron's staff, which represented the tribe of Levi, had not only sprouted with no connection to the earth but budded, blossomed, and this produced what would have been some good tasting almonds. Talk about legitimacy.

As a leader, it is critical that your legitimacy is never brought to question, and results usually are the best answers to these. Do all that you can to protect your legitimacy; everything else, including obedience and followership, finds its relevance and staying power in legitimacy. Just like in the case of Aaron, it puts an end to all grumbling.

- 🔶 36 -

THE EMOTION CALLED ANGER

"Take the staff, and you and your brother Aaron gather the assembly together. Speak to that rock before their eyes and it will pour out its water. You will bring water out of the rock for the community so they and their livestock can drink." Then Moses raised his arm and struck the rock twice with his staff. Water gushed out, and the community and their livestock drank. But the Lord said to Moses and Aaron, "Because you did not trust in me enough to honor me as holy in the sight of the Israelites, you will not bring this community into the land I give them."
—Numbers 20:8, 11, 12, NIV

Many leaders face a myriad of problems when leading others, but I have found that the hardest person to lead is yourself; therefore, self-leadership is the most difficult expression of leadership but is often ignored. One emotion that is often hidden beneath the layers of the character of most individuals is anger. It hardly ever reveals itself until the perfect atmosphere, temperature, and trigger are all lined up for its great reveal.

Moses, like we have indicated, was a meek man, but beneath the leadership cloak was anger waiting to manifest. The children of Israel had complained of the lack of drinking water, precipitated most likely from the burning desert, and out of frustration, exhaustion, and sheer exasperation,

Moses asked God, who gave him explicit instruction on what to do. He was asked to speak to the rock, and water would pour out, but Moses, like a choir conductor, raised his arm and struck the rock twice with his staff. He got the result but lost the most valuable thing, the reward of his exodus—the promised land—because he did not trust God enough to honour him as holy in the eyes of the people.

How many times as leaders have we lost precious things or opportunities due to sometimes misplaced expression of our emotions? While there is a pot purri of emotions present in every leader, I must identify that any leader who seeks to be the best version must seek to master his emotions, especially anger; otherwise, a glass broken often times despite remorse can never be put together again.

- ◈ 37 -

ZEAL

"So Moses said to Israel's judges, "Each of you must put to death those of your people who have yoked themselves to the Baal of Peor." Then an Israelite man brought into the camp a Midianite woman right before the eyes of Moses and the whole assembly of Israel while they were weeping at the entrance to the tent of meeting. When Phinehas son of Eleazar, the son of Aaron, the priest, saw this, he left the assembly, took a spear in his hand and followed the Israelite into the tent. He drove the spear into both of them, right through the Israelite man and into the woman's stomach. Then the plague against the Israelites was stopped; "Phinehas son of Eleazar, the son of Aaron, the priest, has turned my anger away from the Israelites. Since he was as zealous for my honor among them as I am, I did not put an end to them in my zeal."
—Numbers 25:5-8, 11, NIV

"Therefore tell him I am making my covenant of peace with him. He and his descendants will have a covenant of a lasting priesthood, because he was zealous for the honor of his God and made atonement for the Israelites."
— Numbers 25:12, 13, NIV

Zeal, though usually defined by most English dictionaries as a passionate ardour in pursuit of an objective or course of action, in its pure etymology both in Hebrew and Greek, is the word jealous, in this instance with a godly undertone (remember God himself identified as a jealous God in several instances).

If I am permitted, I could define Zeal as passionate jealousy, followed up by a course of action. I am yet to find a succeful leader in the Bible who wasn't consumed by Zeal, and in the verses above, we find a man who heaven not only acknowledged his zeal but gave a lifetime reward.

The children of Israel had done another unthinkable act; despite repeated warnings not to be yoked with the Canaanite women, the men did just that (remember Balaam suggesting to Balak to use women to entice and seduce the sons of Israel earlier). The Israelites began to indulge in sexual immorality with Moabite women who invited them to sacrifice to their gods and yoked themselves to the Baal of Poer. God was angry and instructed Moses that all the leaders would be killed and exposed in broad daylight. A plague was in full effect, and while Moses and the faithful were standing at the entrance of the tent of the meeting, an Israelite staggered into the camp with a strange woman.

The zeal of the Lord "passionate jealousy" consumed Phinehas, son of Eleazar, the son of Aaron, and he took a spear; following the couple, and drove it through them both, causing the plague to cease immediatlely. This was after the death of 24,000 Israelites. His action proved that it is possible a leader's zeal for God turns away negativity.

God immediately acknowledged him, making a convenant of peace, declaring a remembrance for Eleazar and his generation. Godly leaders are always filled with the zeal to perform well; there is a spirit within them that pushes them to go the extra mile in ensuring that a course of action is achieved. While there can be individuals equally driven by a negative zeal, one would understand that it is a quality that is essential to leading.

- ◈ 38 -

DISTRIBUTION OF RESOURCES

"The land is to be allotted to them as an inheritance based on the number of names. To a larger group give a larger inheritance, and to a smaller group a smaller one; each is to receive its inheritance according to the number of those listed. Be sure that the land is distributed by lot. What each group inherits will be according to the names for its ancestral tribe. Each inheritance is to be distributed by lot among the larger and smaller groups."
— Numbers 26:53-56, NIV

Often times a leader may be entrusted with the commonwealth of a business, a people, or even an entire nation, and it is paramount that such an individual is bestowed with the requisite wisdom on the best ways to distribute resources, which in some instances could be limited or sought after by so many. The promise of God was for the Israelites to inherit the entire land mass, and the responsibility to plan the allotment fell on Moses. God was able to advise him on the importance of prioritizing the size of tribes when giving the inheritance; this itself carried profound wisdom if not executed, as the limited land could backfire and lead to rivalry and possible civil war.

As a leader, you must take into account a host of factors, cover your blind sides to guarantee that there is an equitable distribution of resources that can lead to reasonable content by the recipients, do not for a second wish this away, or, more importantly, delegate such a sensitive task, as politics and sentiments may rear their heads, leading to huge dissatisfaction with your leadership.

Many leaders have lost everything on this point alone, due to the alienation of a common sense approach in giving what is due to those who deserve it the most. The example of what the leaders in Israel did and subsequently implemented by the successor of Moses must be emulated to avoid seeds of discontentment, which is commonplace amongst those who have been led. When given a chance, agents of destruction need just a little spark to ignite an inferno. Don't fall for the trap; pay attention to our resources being distributed equitably to the best of your leadership ability.

- ◈ 39 -

EQUITY AND EQUALITY

"The daughters of Zelophehad son of Hepher, the son of Gilead, the son of Makir, the son of Manasseh, belonged to the clans of Manasseh son of Joseph. The names of the daughters were Mahlah, Noah, Hoglah, Milkah and Tirzah. They came forward and stood before Moses, Eleazar the priest, the leaders and the whole assembly at the entrance to the tent of meeting and said, "Our father died in the wilderness. He was not among Korah's followers, who banded together against the Lord, but he died for his own sin and left no sons. Why should our father's name disappear from his clan because he had no son? Give us property among our father's relatives." So Moses brought their case before the Lord, and the Lord said to him, "What Zelophehad's daughters are saying is right. You must certainly give them property as an inheritance among their father's relatives and give their father's inheritance to them."
—Numbers 27:1-7, NIV

"When the Year of Jubilee for the Israelites comes, their inheritance will be added to that of the tribe into which they marry, and their property will be taken from the tribal inheritance of our ancestors."
—Numbers 36:4, NIV

The Jewish tradition is patriarchal in nature, which means the rule of the father, and refers to a social system where men control a disproportionately large share of social, economic, political, and religious power. In such a society, inheritance usually passes down the male line. But the next gem will seek to create some balance.

Equity and equality, are gems every leader must borrow from, considering the times we live in. The daughters of Zelophehad of the clans of Manasseh will redefine existing cultural standpoints and cause a shift of paradigm, which God himself endorsed. The ladies had no father or brothers, and for that reason the risk of their name disappearing from the clan was high. When properties are also to be shared, they would have no stake. Moses took the matter to God, and he agreed that the five daughters must certainly be given property and inheritance just like their male counterparts. This move would have caused ripples in the Israeli heiracherical order where women were often seen and hardly heard.

It is, however, a golden lesson for any leader to adopt, which is to preach and practice godly equality amongst genders. This inclusion will foster good and unlock immense value that exists amongst followers. Everyone wants to feel appreciated and acknowledged; it is not a gender feeling but a human one; therefore, the gem is any leader who can go past age-old traditions by smashing glass ceilings will win unusual loyalty and widespread admiration for such huge risks that yield a significant return on investment. Lead with equity and fairness always, regardless of what preceded you.

- ⬡ 40 -

SUCCESSION

"Moses said to the Lord, "May the Lord, the God who gives breath to all living things, appoint someone over this community to go out and come in before them, one who will lead them out and bring them in, so the Lord's people will not be like sheep without a shepherd." So the Lord said to Moses, "Take Joshua son of Nun, a man in whom is the spirit of leadership, and lay your hand on him."
—Numbers 27:15-18, NIV

"Have him stand before Eleazar the priest and the entire assembly and commission him in their presence."
—Numbers 27:19, NIV

"Give him some of your authority so the whole Israelite community will obey him."
—Numbers 27:20, NIV

"Then he laid his hands on him and commissioned him, as the Lord instructed through Moses."
—Numbers 27:23, NIV

Succession planning is now a catchphrase in modern leadership and management circles for good reasons, but millennia before scripture highlighted the importance of a leader intentionally planning towards what occurs after they have vacated their lofty heights. It is cliché that a good leader or manager's first duty is to prepare for and train his successor. God made it clear that there is a reserved role for leaders in the choice of successors. Joshua was miles ahead of others in his generation beyond the well-known identified instances of spying the promised land and supporting the leader Moses.

My two personal favourites were when Moses left the tent of meeting, and scripture states that Joshua remained in the presence of God, and the second was when he accompanied Moses to climb the mount and possibly at a distance, remaining on the mountain for the same duration of 40 days (he was oblivious to the rebellion in the camp below, when the golden calf was made). So it is little wonder God picked a man who had passed through the tests to climb up to greater responsibilities.

Moses, on the other hand, got specific instructions on passing the baton; one was to have him stand before the priest and the entire assembly and give him an open-air coronation, giving him authority, and laying his hands on him, thus leaving no room for speculation or unfolded ambiguity on who the leader would be.

It is important for leaders, whilst doing the needful, to always handle the necessary, and the selection of a successor is both needful and necessary in nature; picking an individual that understands the demands, has the temperament needed, the political connections, and can guarantee continuity of a vision is critical. Leadership is a continuum, and therefore godly leaders, when they can, must do all they can, not necessarily impose stooges to massage their egos, but ensure they handpick, train, and empower a new generation of leaders. That is the only way a leader can be said to have been truly successful. Succession shouldn't be something like death that is inevitable, but no one wants to discuss it.

- ◈41 -

DIVIDING SPOILS OF VICTORY

"The Lord said to Moses, "You and Eleazar the priest and the family heads of the community are to count all the people and animals that were captured. Divide the spoils equally between the soldiers who took part in the battle and the rest of the community. From the soldiers who fought in the battle, set apart as tribute for the Lord one out of every five hundred, whether people, cattle, donkeys, or sheep. Take this tribute from their half share and give it to Eleazar the priest as the Lord's part."
—Numbers 31:25-29, NIV

One undeniable perk that comes with leadership in many instances must be the spoils of victory. Whether it's a huge bonus or benefits, the leader often times gets the right to choose how hard work is rewarded, and this can be a banana peel for the leader because of the disharmony or the fall out of such decision-making. There was a call to arms, and the Lord instructed vengeance be taken out on the Midianities. Each of the twelve tribe was expected to send a thousand men to battle, along with Phinehas the Priest, alongside articles from the sanctuary and trumpets.

It was a resounding victory leading to the capture of the five Midian Kings and the disgrace of Balaam who was hired to curse the Israelites. The war gave them captives spoils and great plunder. After the ceremonial purification of gold, silver, bronze, iron, tin, lead, and anything that can withstand fire, the next task was for Moses, the leader, to divide the spoils, and you can see that God gave wisdom for this task because of its delicate nature and possible repercussion.

The spoils were counted and shared equally between the soldiers and the rest of the community, and amongst the Levites, etc. The gem we can unearth is that there could well be times you can be in a position to determine how spoils are to be shared. As a leader, take this task in a fair and equitable way, taking into consideration everyone's contribution even when it looks insignificant (Moses rewarded the community who stayed back in camp).

The secret here is to ensure everyone feels like a significant part of the overall success that is being celebrated. This gesture will ensure those following always feel like a part of the overall machinery, ensuring things work according to plan.

- ◈ 42 -

FLEXIBILITY

"Then Moses gave orders about them to Eleazar the priest and Joshua son of Nun and to the family heads of the Israelite tribes. He said to them, "If the Gadites and Reubenites, every man armed for battle, cross over the Jordan with you before the Lord, then when the land is subdued before you, you must give them the land of Gilead as their possession. But if they do not cross over with you armed, they must accept their possession with you in Canaan."
—*Numbers 32:28-30, NIV*

Leadership will always make a demand, often in the form of judgement calls or decisions that may have far-reaching consequences for your leadership and those who follow you. The twelve tribes of Israel were to receive their promised inheritance in Canaan, but two tribes decided to break ranks by making an unusual request that first rattled Moses, who viewed this at first glance as a possible insurrection and flagrant disobedience to God's instructions and will. The tribes of Gad and Reuben approached Moses while the children of Israel were on the east side of the Jordan River waiting to cross over into Cannan. They asked if they could have their own inheritance on the east side because the land looked good for their cattle. Moses understood this needed to be handled with tact; otherwise, it could lead to disharmony and a possible break in rank by the other ten tribes, who could accuse leadership of favouritism;

after all, the reward was to come after the conquest and not before.

One therefore cannot blame Moses for his anger and disposition, but one quality he possessed was a listening ear that naturally precedes the gem of flexibility. Moses therefore, in unequivocal terms, told them that the other tribes would be unhappy if they were unable to join their brothers to conquer the land on the west of the Jordan, facing armies that dwarfed them in numbers already. Also, I personally doubt Moses would have wanted unhappy tribes on his hands as well; he therefore employed flexibility by extracting a promise from the Gadites and Reubenites that every man was to be armed for battle and cross the Jordan; they would be allowed to return to their families and cattle in Gilead after ensuring all their brothers had secured their own inheritance. This was exactly what transpired and led to everyone feeling satisfied.

As leaders, we must never be too rigid in our judgement calls; there must always be some wriggle room to accommodate some certain unforeseen situations, circumstances, and requests. Godly leaders are flexible in nature, always avoiding hubris standing in the way, instead seeking novel ways to ensure everyone to a degree has their view points considered and, when doable, accommodated. Remain flexible as a leader; it will grant you the ability to stretch beyond measure.

- 💎 43 -

VISION EXECUTORS

"These are the names of the men who are to assign the land for you as an inheritance: Eleazar the priest and Joshua son of Nun. And appoint one leader from each tribe to help assign the land."
—Numbers 34:17-18, NIV

Visions are sometimes overwhelming; even those who birth them may not have the capabilities and capacity to nurse them to adulthood; therefore, for every leader, the presence of vision executors is instrumental to their success. In previous gems we had indicated the promise of Canaan, and Moses had marshalled out the vision, but he needed men to see it to fruition. There needed to be assignors to the land who would guarantee that every tribe got its alloacaion, and certain individuals had to be tasked with that assignment, including the priest, Joshua, and a representative leader from each tribe, all vision executors.

The obvious gem is that as a leader you must have on your team vision executors who understand their unique role in actualizing something much bigger than themselves. Leaders must identify the cream of the crop to bring to reality the vision you have painted; they must be well invested in the dream and have a portion of your spirit working in them to execute. A leader must therefore continually in his daily dealings look out for this scarce human resource of executors; only then can he boast of peace all around to concentrate on other strategic thought processes and implementation. Many leaders are bugged down by the micro-management of every single element of the vision they carry in their hearts; the negative consequences usually override any positives. Godly leaders find followers who are capable of crossing the finish line.

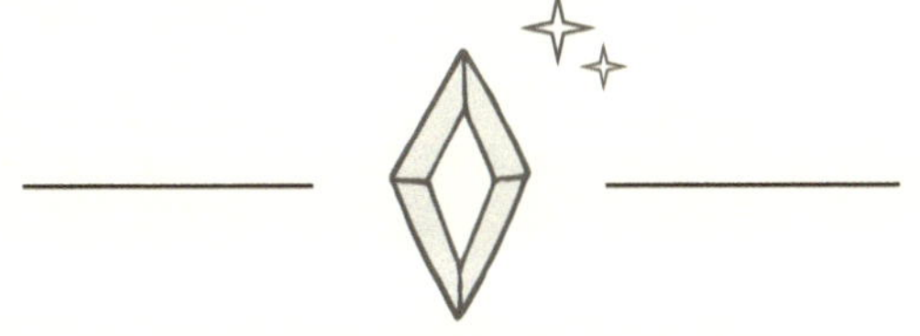

THE BOOK OF
DEUTERONOMY

- ◈ 44 -

TAKING ACTION

"The Lord our God said to us at Horeb, "You have stayed long enough at this mountain. Break camp and advance into the hill country of the Amorites; go to all the neighboring peoples in the Arabah, in the mountains, in the western foothills, in the Negev and along the coast, to the land of the Canaanites and to Lebanon, as far as the great river, the Euphrates. See, I have given you this land. Go in and take possession of the land the Lord swore he would give to your fathers—to Abraham, Isaac and Jacob—and to their descendants after them."
—Deuteronomy 1:6-8, NIV

Many leaders suffer from what I may describe as paralysis in taking action, which is dangerous and can backfire on several fronts if not overcome. The main thrust for any leader is taking action; imagine what would become of a company or even nation cursed with a leader who is adept at not taking necessary action. The Israelites had been moving around now for years; their feet had never gotten swollen, the clothes had no tear, bellies filled with Manna; they had become complacent in taking possession of the land according to God's predetermined timetable. At Horeb, God gave Moses, their leader, a crucial command: move. Their camp had stayed at that mountain too long; they needed to disperse and advance into the land he promised their patriarchs.

The key lesson here is that you can only take possession if you first take action. The promises made to them were intangible and could only become tangible through physical progress. As a leader, you must fiercely oppose any paralysis that may engulf those under your leadership and insist on them taking action. It may be expansion or growth plans lying down in architectural plans; it may be unfinished projects; whatever the size or the magnitude, it will never be done except you lead the people to take action; in fact, God frowns at this static position and chastised the children of Israel for not taking necessary action to fulfil his word.

If you are a leader, you may not always get it right in all your decisions or actions, but a leader who fails after taking action, is a hundred times better than one who does nothing; therefore, imbibe a spirit of taking steps that leads to your own desired promise land; do not let fear, failure, anxiety, or anything else freeze you into a statute mode. Leaders are called to act; leaders are called to take action.

- ◈ 45 -

RECOLLECTION OF EVENTS

"Only be careful, and watch yourselves closely so that you do not forget the things your eyes have seen or let them fade from your heart as long as you live. Teach them to your children and to their children after them."
—*Deuteronomy 4:9, NIV*

In high School, sitting in my government class, I particularly loved history; the richness of the past offered me an escape to travel to lands in time past while still seated at my desk. While history holds significant relevance for us, elders also utilize it as a tool to maintain the faith and hope of those who follow them. Moses advocated that the nation of Israel never forgets their history and to continually call on past events; that way, they are able to mirror their present decision-making at that moment to give a predictable outcome.

A good leader understands that the grounds of the past are littered with the decisions of those who preceded them, and it is too much of a gamble and risk toying with the lives and destiny of those you are called to lead. Leaders should constantly entrench the past in their dealings; it can offer an advantage like no other. This tradition will be responsible in the case of the Israelites when they would have kings to be able to find their way back to the track of holiness when the covenant with their fathers was remembered. Such kings were a success, and those who deliberated or unintentionally ignored the price paid a huge price in return.

Godly leaders with wisdom constantly advocate for the recollection of past events in order to guarantee a glorious future of prosperity and gratitude amongst those they lead and themselves.

- ◇ 46 -

CAUTION IN YOUR PLACE OF REST

"See, I am setting before you today a blessing and a curse— the blessing if you obey the commands of the Lord your God that I am giving you today; the curse if you disobey the commands of the Lord your God and turn from the way that I command you today by following other gods, which you have not known. When the Lord your God has brought you into the land you are entering to possess, you are to proclaim on Mount Gerizim the blessings, and on Mount Ebal the curses."
—Deuteronomy 11:26-29, NIV

A Japanese saying goes like this: "At the moment of victory, tighten the straps of your helmet. Nothing provides greater temptation to leaders than complacency when they have met their set goals, when in essence it is the time to be most cautious. Many bible commentators have often spoken about the life of a future king of Israel, Solomon; his ability to indulge in excesses and pleasure was borne out of a season of unrivalled peace, prosperity, and rest. Countries that heavily rely on philosophy, the arts, music, and other cultural expressions tend to be at peace, but they often suffer from complacency, which can lead to forgetting the struggle and succumbing to excesses that ultimately bring down people.

After God informed Moses that he wouldn't be able to enter Canaan, he delivered a series of last-minute warnings to the nation. He stressed the importance of rest and cautioned against succumbing to the temptations of neighbouring countries and their vices. He understood the potential consequences of a period of rest, which could lead to blindness, albeit not literally; it can dull senses and distort perceptions.

Every time a leader achieves a set goal or reaches a place of rest, he must seek and find caution. A leader's job is never truly done, and while those you lead may find the leeway, leaders don't possess the luxury of letting down their guard but ensuring that they themselves and others find caution so as not to stray into unknown territory or into the hands of their foes, who prepare mostly for battles when a man is at rest.

Therefore, dear leader, when the Lord guides you, never place yourself in a situation where you are unable to promptly respond to any existential threat to your leadership and those under your guidance.

- ◈ 47 -

CRITERIA FOR LEADERSHIP

"The king, moreover, must not acquire great numbers of horses for himself or make the people return to Egypt to get more of them, for the Lord has told you, "You are not to go back that way again." He must not take many wives, or his heart will be led astray. He must not accumulate large amounts of silver and gold. When he takes the throne of his kingdom, he is to write for himself on a scroll a copy of this law, taken from that of the Levitical priests. It is to be with him, and he is to read it all the days of his life so that he may learn to revere the Lord his God and follow carefully all the words of this law and these decrees and not consider himself better than his fellow Israelites and turn from the law to the right or to the left. Then he and his descendants will reign a long time over his kingdom in Israel."
—Deuteronomy 17:16-20 NIV

All forms of leadership demand criteria for anyone to occupy a leadership position; countries, for instance, have a list of conditions that must be met for anyone to become a Governor, Prime Minister, or President; businesses have a clear set of qualities that those who govern their affairs must possess; this is without saying, emphasizing the importance of laid-down rules to separate the tares from the wheat when it comes to individuals jostling to lead.

Through prophetic insight, Moses was close to going to sleep and knew that a season would come in the life of the young nation where they would want to be like their neighbours and desire a king instead of a judge over their affairs. He systematically laid down criteria for leadership. I find it very instructive. The first thing he advised was not to have a leader who would go on a spending spree to acquire great horses for himself, i.e., pushing for prudent men. Current leaders live like emperors at the expense of their constituents.

The second point he made was to steer clear of a man who takes on an excessive number of wives, as this often leads to instability and a constant pull in different directions, which in turn impacts his decision-making and ultimately his leadership. Thirdly, such a leader should not be a conceited individual who is primarily interested in amassing the vast wealth of all those under his guidance.

Finally, such a person must be a man of the word, steadfastly adhering to its teachings and keeping them close to his heart and lips. This will ensure that he maintains humility before God and others, a quality he concludes will ensure his longevity. In analyzing this recommendation, I have studied hundreds of leaders in and out of scripture to advocate that the advice given is sound and timeless. To lead effectively, any potential or current leader must seek to adopt these criteria.

- ◈ 48 -

OPEN ENDORSEMENT

"Then Moses summoned Joshua and said to him in the presence of all Israel, "Be strong and courageous, for you must go with this people into the land that the Lord swore to their ancestors to give them, and you must divide it among them as their inheritance. The Lord himself goes before you and will be with you; he will never leave you nor forsake you. Do not be afraid; do not be discouraged."
—Deuteronomy 31:7-8 NIV

There is a correlation between the acceptance of any leader and the open endorsement of a worthy predecessor. In our modern world, we see how much political capital such an action carries. I will often argue that, though change is beneficial, when a beneficial leader exits the picture, people want continuity and the assurance that it provides.

Moses understood this on several occasions, bringing Joshua's achievements to the open assembly and publicly charging him with his responsibilities to God and those he led. Many great empires and business conglomerates have collapsed due to the failure of their often successful leaders to not only identify worthy protégés or external successors but also to openly endorse them. This failure, more importantly, led to doubts among the public about the authenticity of such endorsements. The adage "nature abhors a vacuum" also applies to leadership positions.

A leader must, when possible, never leave in doubt who he wants to take over the reins of power and authority. God gave Jesus Christ an open endorsement before all creation, the authority he was to possess across the realms; there was not a shadow of doubt if He indeed was the son of God sent to redeem mankind.

- ◊ 49 -

LEGACY

"Since then, no prophet has risen in Israel like Moses, whom the Lord knew face to face, who did all those signs and wonders the Lord sent him to do in Egypt— to Pharaoh and to all his officials and to his whole land. For no one has ever shown the mighty power or performed the awesome deeds that Moses did in the sight of all Israel."
—Deuteronomy 34:10-12 NIV

When the curtains are drawn, all that counts are your deeds and actions to be tested by the rough winds of time; nothing else will matter than the legacy left behind. Whether consciously or otherwise, Moses invested in his assignment to such a degree that it was never in doubt that he was called and heavily helped by God. The Bible acknowledges that no prophet has ever risen like Moses, who performed signs and wonders and whom God knew face-to-face. It concludes that no one has ever shown the mighty power or performed the awesome deeds that he did in front of Israel, underscoring the importance for every leader to be what I would like to call legacy conscious. In a state where a leader acts with the consciousness of his works speaking for him when he no longer has a voice of defence, whether that voice is taken by death, power exchange, or any other factor, the deeds of the leader when scrutinized by others are given favourable commendation for acting selflessly and most importantly mightily for the greater good, often at great expense and sacrifice.

Leaders must be serious about the long-lasting impact of the key decisions and actions that they undertake in the present and their relative impact in the future. Usually, the ultimate evaluation of your leadership success doesn't occur during your tenure but rather after you step down. It's in retrospect that the passage of time weighs and measures your decisions, defining you as a good or bad leader.

It is always difficult to make this distinction in the present moment due to the movement and volatility of evens that may hoodwink individuals to make an authentic judgement call, but leaders fall victim and get carried away by sycophants and yes, men who sing their praises to the heavens. The gem is to be conscious that you make the present count to enable the future stand and applaud.

THE BOOK OF

JOSHUA

- ◈ 50 -

RECIPE FOR LEADERSHIP EXPLOITS

"Keep this Book of the Law always on your lips; meditate on it day and night, so that you may be careful to do everything written in it. Then you will be prosperous and successful."
—Joshua 1:8, NIV

Joshua had just taken over the reins of leadership; he had a first-row view of the challenges his predecessor Moses encountered leading a tough and sinful nation; he knew the stakes were high; so much of God's agenda for redemption for mankind rested on the nation of Israel. The Lord would then speak to him and provide the recipe for the leadership exploits we now study in the life of this faithful lieutenant.

The gem is simple yet profound. First, he was expected as a leader to keep the book of the law always on his lips, not once in a while but always, and also to meditate on it and finally do what was written; this way he was guaranteed prosperity and success.

The three elements in this approach are the use of spoken words, mental reflection, and action. This forum can be replicated even to this very day. The Lord himself promised that a leader who consistently speaks about the word will refrain from making mistakes, instead would elevate others and praise God. Therefore, the first area to focus on is the mouth; the next is the mind; a leader who consistently meditates will undoubtedly yield commendable results; and lastly, the leader's actions will undoubtedly lead to success, as their mouth and mind have adequately prepared them to take actions that will undoubtedly bring prosperity.

- ✦ 51 -

PROMPTNESS TO ACT

"Go through the camp and tell the people, 'Get your provisions ready. Three days from now you will cross the Jordan here to go in and take possession of the land the Lord your God is giving you for your own."
—Joshua 1:11, NIV

I've seen many leaders suffer from what I call leadership action paralysis. In this situation, a leader is capable of articulating all necessary tasks and possesses the necessary resources, including the team, but faces a significant challenge: he is unable to activate the ignition and push the accelerator pedal. Many reasons can be attributed when a leader fails to act, but one is guaranteed: inaction will guarantee no outcome.

Joshua, the newly minted leader of the Israelites, now in the driver's seat, was instructed by the Lord of the significance of prompt action. I presume Joshua recollected several episodes when the people failed to take action; he understood that his promptness to act would keep the momentum going, and the instruction was direct and definite for the people to prepare themselves and provisions because in three days they would cross the Jordan and take possession of the promised land.

This gem highlights the crucial characteristic of godly leaders who act promptly; God Himself, is always on time, consistently delivering results. Do not be a leader who fiddles away, second-guessing instructions that affect your life, family, and those you lead. Delay can be extremely dangerous in many regards, leading to irrecoverable losses and damage. If you are called to lead, you must be prompt in taking actions.

One of the downsides of delayed action is the tendency to water things down. Once an instruction is still bright red hot, take action promptly.

- ◈ 52 -

KEEP YOUR WORD

*"The seventh time around, when the priests sound-
ed the trumpet blast, Joshua commanded the army,
"Shout! For the Lord has given you the city! The city
and all that is in it are to be devoted to the Lord. Only
Rahab the prostitute and all who are with her in her
house shall be spared, because she hid the spies we
sent."*
—Joshua 6:16-17, NIV

*"Joshua said to the two men who had spied out the
land, "Go into the prostitute's house and bring her
out and all who belong to her, in accordance with
your oath to her." So the young men who had done
the spying went in and brought out Rahab, her father
and mother, her brothers and sisters and all who belonged to her. They brought out her entire family and
put them in a place outside the camp of Israel."*
—Joshua 6:22-23, NIV

Whether in the home, church, community, or marketplace,
keeping one's word serves as a medium of exchange
between leaders and those under your leadership. It's
crucial for godly leaders to value this gem, as trust fosters
relationships and God values human relationships deeply.
Joshua proved again that keeping one's word is the
hallmark of a godly leader. He dispatched two men to
spy on the land of Jericho, which God had promised the
Israelites; the inhabitants were filled with fear. A prostitute

named Rahab discovered the spies' presence and had to hide them, ensuring their safety by providing lodging. By exercising faith, she extracted a promise from the spies that she and her household would be spared from the invasion and destruction that was to come on Jericho.

When the walls of the city came crashing down, I can imagine that in the middle of a fierce battle the leader still remembered that his spies had given their word to a prostitute; he would declare that she and all who belonged to her be brought out in accordance with the oath made to her and put in a place outside the camp of Israel. God justified her as righteous due to her faith, making the story even more intriguing. Matthew's genealogy of Jesus Christ mentions her as one of five women, and Hebrews 11 lists her among the faith champions in the Pantheon of Faith Greats. Before I get carried away by how God is so intentional, all of these were made possible because Joshua kept his word. Are you an aspiring or accomplished leader? It pays to always keep your word.

- ◈ 53 -

WATCH THOSE YOU LEAD CLOSELY

"But the Israelites were unfaithful in regard to the devoted things; Achan son of Karmi, the son of Zimri, the son of Zerah, of the tribe of Judah, took some of them. So the Lord's anger burned against Israel."
—Joshua 7:1, NIV

"The Lord said to Joshua, "Stand up! What are you doing down on your face? Israel has sinned; they have violated my covenant, which I commanded them to keep. They have taken some of the devoted things; they have stolen, they have lied, they have put them with their own possessions. That is why the Israelites cannot stand against their enemies; they turn their backs and run because they have been made liable to destruction. I will not be with you anymore unless you destroy whatever among you is devoted to destruction."
—Joshua 7:10-12, NIV

Joshua was in great despair; he hated the taste of defeat. Now Joshua was already winning a reputation as a military commander, and his target was the city of Ai. His scouts reported what would be an overwhelming Israelite victory, electing a few thousand to go up to fight and not the entire army. What was meant to be an assured victory turned out to be defeat. Thirty-six men were killed, and the others chased to quarries and struck. The people meted in fear and became without form like water. What could have gone wrong? Joshua wondered, tearing his clothes and facedown before the ark for a day.

He questioned God on how his army was routed by the enemies. The Lord, in a quick rebuke, asked the leader to stand up, saying that one of this men had stolen devoted things, making everyone else liable to destruction. Joshua and his commanders had not watched those they led closely. Joshua understood that God was a jealous God, and top on his list was his total disdain for idolatry and things dedicated to a worthless god.

A certain man by the name Achan was identified as the culprit after the lenses were narrowed to his family. Out of greed during the plunder, he stole a robe from Babylonia, two hundred shekels of silver, and a bar of gold weighing fifty shekels; he had them hidden in the ground inside his tent. The punishment was swift, with him, his family, animals, and stolen goods stoned to death, leading to God's anger turning away.

Dear leader, are you keeping watch over those you lead closely? This gem reminds leaders of the immutable fact that many times the actions of their subordinates have a far-reaching effect on their leadership. You must install monitoring mechanisms, not necessarily to micromanage but to share that you have your eyes on what is being done under your leadership. One man's error was responsible for the defeat of an entire army. Keep tabs and watch those you lead closely.

- ◈ 54 -

DISCERNMENT

"However, when the people of Gibeon heard what Joshua had done to Jericho and Ai, they resorted to a ruse: They went as a delegation whose donkeys were loaded with worn-out sacks and old wineskins, cracked and mended. They put worn and patched sandals on their feet and wore old clothes. All the bread in their food supply was dry and moldy. Then they went to Joshua in the camp at Gilgal and said to him and the Israelites, "We have come from a distant country; make a treaty with us."
—Joshua 9:3-6, NIV

"The Israelites sampled their provisions but did not enquire of the Lord. Then Joshua made a treaty of peace with them to let them live, and the leaders of the assembly ratified it by oath."
—Joshua 9:14-15, NIV

The fame of the Israelites had gone far; nations all around the promised land heard of how a certain God was fighting for them, how He defeated the Pharaoh and totally destroyed Egypt, how He brought down the walls of the ancient city of Jericho without a single arrow fired, how He delivered Ai into their hands, along with the two Amorite Kings: Sihon and Og. A certain town called Gibeon had shrewd leaders who hatched a plan to divert the impending doom from the trajectory of their country. The ruse involved them dressing rundown and appearing like they came from far away seeking a treaty with Joshua.

In the momentary absence of discernment, Joshua and the elders agreed and made a treaty of peace to let them live, ratified by oath. The deception was now complete; the Israelites were not discerning and did not enquire of the Lord. Three days later, they discovered the Gibeonites were their neighbours, and the people grumbled against their leaders for falling for a cheap trick. Rather than being destroyed, they became woodcutters and water carriers to the Israelites which wasn't God's intention to sanitize the land of its inhabitants.

The gem here for leaders is to always be discerning; it is so important that its absence can lead to failure and even death for such an individual. Godly leaders, with the help of the Holy Spirit, can seek out the gift and exercise it; its constant use leads to greater accuracy. All leaders must therefore endeavour to see that they are discerning in all they do and commit to avoid being deceived by trickery.

- ◈ 55 -

FAITH OF GREAT PROPORTIONS

"On the day the Lord gave the Amorites over to Israel, Joshua said to the Lord in the presence of Israel: "Sun, stand still over Gibeon, and you, moon, over the Valley of Aijalon." So the sun stood still, and the moon stopped, till the nation avenged itself on its enemies, as it is written in the Book of Jashar. The sun stopped in the middle of the sky and delayed going down about a full day. There has never been a day like it before or since—a day when the Lord listened to a human being. Surely the Lord was fighting for Israel!"
—*Joshua 10:12-14, NIV*

An eclipse occurred while writing this book in April of 2024. I was glued to my television screen watching one of God's cosmic shows on full display to the inhabitants of the earth; no mortal was able to start or end it, all in the sovereign palms of Jehovah. This event was not the first time in human history that the constellations displayed great signs in the heavens; in one instance, the event was actually triggered by the faith action of a mortal man. The five kings of the Amorites—the kings of Jerusalem—joined forces to attack Gibeon after hearing their truce with Israel, seeing that Gibeon was an important city and larger than Ai and all its men were even good fighters. An SOS was sent to Joshua by the Gibeonites requesting military assistance.

After an all-night march, Joshua took the invading forces by surprise, and the Lord threw the enemy's camp into confusion, and as they fled, He opened his warehouse of fighting arsenal, hurling down large hailstones on them, doing more damage than the sword. On that day, it is recorded that Joshua said to the Lord in the presence of all Israel for the sun to stand still over Gibeon and moon, over the Valley of Aijalon, until he avenged the enemies. Every time I brood over this specific tale, the sheer audacity, better described as faith shown by Joshua, blows my socks off my feet.

Leaders must exhibit unusual high readings on the faith meter—while not enough to control celestial bodies, as it records that there has never been a day like it before or since when God listened to a human being. But there are other areas in the leadership journey that require our radical faith in tough situations; when confronted with tough scenarios, it is not enough to cower in the corner. Joshua rode all night, fought multiple kings, and controlled the two major stars in the sky, powered by the fuel of faith all in a day's job.

Godly leaders are faith agents whose faith supply levels are never low; you can imagine the seal on Joshua's leadership credentials with this action. The gem is to lead in a manner worthy of honour and reverence; faith and its results will connect you with those you lead, providing a precedent for all to draw inspiration from.

- ✦ 56 -

COMPLETENESS OF MISSION

"Now the five kings had fled and hidden in the cave at Makkedah. When Joshua was told that the five kings had been found hiding in the cave at Makkedah, he said, "Roll large rocks up to the mouth of the cave, and post some men there to guard it. But don't stop; pursue your enemies! Attack them from the rear and don't let them reach their cities, for the Lord your God has given them into your hand."
— Joshua 10:16-19, NIV

"So Joshua subdued the whole region, including the hill country, the Negev, the western foothills, and the mountain slopes, together with all their kings. He left no survivors. He totally destroyed all who breathed, just as the Lord, the God of Israel, had commanded. Joshua subdued them from Kadesh Barnea to Gaza and from the whole region of Goshen to Gibeon. All these kings and their lands Joshua conquered in one campaign because the Lord, the God of Israel, fought for Israel. Then Joshua returned with all Israel to the camp at Gilgal."
—Joshua 10:40-43, NIV

"As the Lord commanded his servant Moses, so Moses commanded Joshua, and Joshua did it; he left nothing undone of all that the Lord commanded Moses."
—Joshua 11:15, NIV

Leaders understand that the job is only done when it is done. Joshua, after the previous act of going down in history as the only human God ever listened to in freezing the celestial bodies that mark times and seasons, secured what could be best described as a landslide victory and did not relent or rest on his oars. The five kings he fought had fled and hidden in a cave. When he was informed that the kings had been found, his instructions were definite in nature; large rocks were to be rolled to cover up the mouth of the cave and even posted men to guard it. Even at that, he instructed his men to not stop but pursue the enemies, attacking them from the rear and not allowing them to reach their cities.

He would still prove that leaders complete the mission at whatever cost, when while subduing the hill country, the Negev, he executed God's command in ensuring that he left no survivors and destroyed all who breathed, subduing them all in a single campaign. Only until this was done did he return to camp at Gilgal. Leaders who are achievers only call it quits at the end of accomplishing all they set out to achieve, not at the start, not at the middle, only at the very end of it. Godly leaders must understand that God's expectation of leadership is with the mindset of completeness of mission; the mission must never be aborted; it must be fought for until completion. The gem is having a mission-complete approach towards all your dealings.

- ◈ 58 -

VOW KEEPING

"Then Joshua summoned the Reubenites, the Gadites and the half-tribe of Manasseh and said to them, "You have done all that Moses the servant of the Lord commanded, and you have obeyed me in everything I commanded. For a long time now—to this very day— you have not deserted your fellow Israelites but have carried out the mission the Lord your God gave you. Now that the Lord your God has given them rest as he promised, return to your homes in the land that Moses the servant of the Lord gave you on the other side of the Jordan."
—Joshua 22:1-4, NIV

The Children of Israel had shown so much rebellion that Moses must have thought he had another in his hands. They were heading for Canaan; before they crossed the River Jordan, the tribes of Reuben, Gad, and the half tribe of Manasseh elected to stake their claim and chose to settle east of the Jordan; this was primarily due to large herds and flocks, and they saw the land prime for raising livestock. Moses was initially against the thought of tribes splitting up, assuming it was a ploy to avoid fighting, but they collectively made a pledge proposing that they build pens and homes for their families, while the men arm themselves to fight and will only return back when all the other tribes have succeeded in securing their portions in the promised land.

This pledge was accepted, and Moses gave them the land east of the Jordan. Several years down the line after the death of Moses, Joshua would like all godly leaders to honour the vow made by his predecessor. He gave them his blessings, and they returned to their homes. Often times we see leaders unable to keep their own vows, how much more those of predecessors for whatever reason, but godly leaders honour god and moral vows made to others; they understand this breeds an unbreakable bond. The gem is to keep all vows made.

- ◈ 59 -

QUICK TO QUELL
ANY POTENTIAL TROUBLE

"When Phinehas the priest and the leaders of the community—the heads of the clans of the Israelites—heard what Reuben, Gad and Manasseh had to say, they were pleased. And Phinehas son of Eleazar, the priest, said to Reuben, Gad and Manasseh, "Today we know that the Lord is with us, because you have not been unfaithful to the Lord in this matter. Now you have rescued the Israelites from the Lord's hand."
—Joshua 22:30-31, NIV

A standout quality for God-fearing leaders is their uncanny ability to quell any potential trouble seen on the horizon. It is an indispensable ingredient in the leadership cookbook; people will bring along what they perceive to be right or wrong actions. In our previous gem we learnt how the tribes of Reuben, Gad, and Manneseh had the vow made by Moses kept by Joshua, who blessed them and sent them with great wealth—large herds of livestock, silver, gold, bronze, iron, and clothing—but upon their return they did something quite interesting; they built an imposing altar there by the Jordan for fear of heavenly judgement, and that triggered anger in the camps of the other tribes as the whole assembly gathered at Shiloh to go to war with their brother tribes.

A civil war in the history of the young nation was something no one wanted. But rather than take up arms, Joshua and the Israelites sent Phinehas, son of the High Priest, along with representatives from each tribe to enquire first. Upon arrival, they questioned the motive behind such an action. The host tribes were quick to calm frayed nerves, saying that their actions was not to turn away from God and to burn offerings (,) but just as a form of historic landmark, a witness whereby in the future, descendants may seek to exclude them from the commonwealth of Israel, saying the Jordan is a boundary and the Reubenites and Gadites have no share in the Lord; they can point to the replica.

The visiting priest and leaders heard the word and were pleased and reported to the Israelites who became glad to hear the report and praise God, and the talk of waging a devastating war was extinguished. Every leader must be quick to see afar off when and where potential trouble may be brewing, and before extreme action is undertaken, must invest in diplomatic effort to quell such trouble before they come home to roost. The gem is that godly leaders do not hesitate to quell trouble; they know the potential destruction that awaits when you turn the other way.

- 💠 60 -

SPIRITUAL STAND

"But if serving the Lord seems undesirable to you, then choose for yourselves this day whom you will serve, whether the gods your ancestors served beyond the Euphrates, or the gods of the Amorites, in whose land you are living. But as for me and my household, we will serve the Lord."
— Joshua 24:15, NIV

Growing up, this must have been one of the earliest verses I must have been exposed to and still remains one of the most iconic declarations of faith in Christian households all around the world. Joshua understood that his spiritual stand made a lot of difference and had a significant influence on those he was leading. He stood in the assembly and publicly registered his faith position, something a number of modern leaders shy away from to avoid isolating a section of those they lead; they compromise and are unable to make public declarations on which God they answer to, and in the process, in a bid to please men, they displease the one who gave them the leadership in the first instance.

He made it clear that even if he were the last man standing, he and his immediate household would serve the Lord. This is an indication that godly leaders must never be ashamed, shy, or arrogant to ensure that at every point in time everyone knows their conviction and spiritual stand.

It is better as a leader to lose face in front of mortals than to lose face in front of an immortal. The gem here is that leaders know that leadership is a trust from God, and at all times, their constant sincerity (not the public image version for the press and public) is worn on their sleeves with reverence and humility.

The gem here is that godly leaders must take a spiritual stand. My question for you is, are you ready?

- ◈ 61 -

RECORD KEEPING

"And Joshua recorded these things in the Book of the Law of God. Then he took a large stone and set it up there under the oak near the holy place of the Lord."
—Joshua 24:26, NIV

In my extensive years of studying leaders from every conceivable strata of human existence captured through human history, one quality stands out and is even more evident in the Bible, and that is that good leaders are good record keepers. When the covenant between God and Israel was renewed at Shechem, in the presence of all the tribes, elders, leaders, judges, and officials, after the extensive rendition of God's favour, deliverance, provision, and protection of his chosen people, the decrees and laws were reaffirmed, but one gem that stood out was that Joshua recorded these things in the book of the Law of God.

People record different things for various reasons, often to serve as a reminder, others as a witness, but whatever the rationale behind it, good leaders are good record keepers. They can then ensure that they leave a trove of wisdom and knowledge, coupled with key historical facts, for their people and future leaders. In all the leadership positions I have personally occupied, it is mandatory for me to record my stewardship for posterity sake; often, I also rely on it to draw strength in seasons of doubt and worry. If you want to be a godly leader who will lead well, you must adopt the culture of keeping records. It will also ensure your affairs are well organized, in order, as they can also be called upon either when you remain on the leadership saddle or after vacating the stage. The gem here is to keep good records for the sake of today and most especially for the unknown tomorrow.

THE BOOK OF
JUDGES

- ◈ 62 -

VACUUM

> *"Then the Lord raised up judges, who saved them out of the hands of these raiders. Whenever the Lord raised up a judge for them, he was with the judge and saved them out of the hands of their enemies as long as the judge lived; for the Lord relented because of their groaning under those who oppressed and afflicted them."*
> —*Judges 2:16, 18, NIV*

There must and should not be a vacuum when it comes to leadership. Leaders need to understand and appreciate their role in the grand scheme of things; this foreknowledge should be an impetus for them to deliver. The Children of Israel were neck deep in trouble; they had raiding parties who were causing havoc to lives and property. They had violated God's express laws by an inexcusable compromise; they also engaged in unholy alliances through marriage. The conduct was nothing short of incorrigible and led to them being subjected to enemies. It is at this instance, upon supplication to the Lord, that he had to send a deliverer to save them, and what did he do? He raised leaders. The verse says he raised up judges who saved the Israelites out of the hands of their enemies.

Those who often question the necessity of leaders must understand that the absence of godly leaders is an invitation to lack of direction, chaos, and trouble. Leaders must appreciate that they were called to fix a vacuum; the right leader is a deliverer who holds the capacity to lead others to a season of peace and prosperity. I have seen leaders who suffer from the dreaded imposters syndrome, and it is of necessity that godly leaders establish their necessity, but internally and eternally. The world needs godly leaders, the church needs godly leaders, and the market place needs godly leaders. The gem for leaders is to appreciate that they are a necessary fill-up in areas of vacuum to bring deliverance to others.

- 💎 63 -

GET IT DONE YOURSELF

"Again the Israelites cried out to the Lord, and he gave them a deliverer—Ehud, a left-handed man, the son of Gera the Benjamite. The Israelites sent him with tribute to Eglon king of Moab. Now Ehud had made a double-edged sword about a cubit long, which he strapped to his right thigh under his clothing. He presented the tribute to Eglon king of Moab, who was a very fat man. After Ehud had presented the tribute, he sent on their way those who had carried it. But on reaching the stone images near Gilgal he himself went back to Eglon and said, "Your Majesty, I have a secret message for you." The king said to his attendants, "Leave us!" And they all left. Ehud then approached him while he was sitting alone in the upper room of his palace and said, "I have a message from God for you." As the king rose from his seat, Ehud reached with his left hand, drew the sword from his right thigh and plunged it into the king's belly. Even the handle sank in after the blade, and his bowels discharged. Ehud did not pull the sword out, and the fat closed in over it. Then Ehud went out to the porch; he shut the doors of the upper room behind him and locked them. After he had gone, the servants came and found the doors of the upper room locked. They said, "He must be relieving himself in the inner room of the palace." They waited to the point of embarrassment, but when he did not open the doors of the room, they took a key and unlocked them. There they saw their Lord fallen to the floor, dead."
— *Judges 3.15 25, NIV*

Nothing beats a movie with a nice protagonist, a shrewd attitude, and a knack for things done by themselves. We can learn a valuable lesson from the story of Ehud about the importance of leaders possessing or demonstrating shrewd judgment in their actions. The King of Moab, known as Elong, chose him to carry and sing a tribute, but he had a secret agenda; he had made a decision to act and create a conflict. After the tribute presentation and departure of others, he returned seeking a private audience with the King, who foolishly dismissed his attendant. Ehud sensed the opportunity, and approached the King, claiming to have a message from God. When the King arose, Ehud plunged the sword into the mass of flesh, causing even the handle to sink in with the entire sword. Immediately, he fled, and the king discovered dead much later

I particularly admire the audacity with which Ehud first demonstrated his shrewd plans of smuggling in a weapon, his ploy to return, and his bravery in carrying out the task himself. Modern leaders, in my opinion, refrain from confronting the opposition head-on. Instead, we should embrace the knowledge that leaders who (we) remember and celebrate often take the initiative to accomplish tasks independently. They are unafraid to take on challenging tasks when others fail to step up. Godly leaders must appreciate the gem or answer any clarion call to getting things done by themselves; this significantly increases any leader's value in the eyes of those he leads.

- 💎 64 -

HONOR FLOWS TOWARDS BOLD ACTION

"Barak said to her, "If you go with me, I will go; but if you don't go with me, I won't go." "Certainly I will go with you," said Deborah. "But because of the course you are taking, the honor will not be yours, for the Lord will deliver Sisera into the hands of a woman. So Deborah went with Barak to Kedesh."
—Judges 4:8, 9, NIV

"Villagers in Israel would not fight; they held back until I, Deborah, arose, until I arose, a mother in Israel. God chose new leaders when war came to the city gates, but not a shield or spear was seen among forty thousand in Israel."
— Judges 5:7, 8, NIV

"Most blessed of women be Jael, the wife of Heber the Kenite, most blessed of tent-dwelling women. He asked for water, and she gave him milk; in a bowl fit for nobles she brought him curdled milk. Her hand reached for the tent peg, her right hand for the workman's hammer. She struck Sisera, she crushed his head, she shattered and pierced his temple. At her feet he sank, he fell; there he lay. At her feet he sank, he fell; where he sank, there he fell—dead.
— Judges 5:24-27, NIV

No man can bestow honor on himself; it is something a secondary party must exercise in order for it to carry both value and merit. Also another gem is that honour flows naturally and unhindered towards leaders who take bold actions and not those who shy away from esponsibilities. After the left-handed Ehud died, the children of Israel were terrorised by the kings of Canaan, and were led by a female prophet called Deborah. She held court and summoned a man by the name Barak, giving him heavenly instructions to take on Sisera, the commander of the opposing army, a golden opportunity for honour for any soldier, but instead of taking the bull by the horns, he gave a condition that he would only go if Deborah followed, and she famously declared, "Certainly I will go with you, but because of the course you are taking, the honour will not be yours, for the Lord will deliver Sisera into the hands of a woman."

The honour of most fighting generals is to be the ones who took down or held captive their opposite number something that was not lost on Barak. That day God gave victory, as he promised, but the honour did not flow towards Barak despite chasing Sisera and his troops after the routing by the Lord. Sisera on foot fled to the tent of a woman called Jael, who, under the pretence of providing the much-needed cover for the fleeing soldier, picked up a tent peg and hammer, driving it into the general's temple while he slept. At that point, Barak came in and was shown where Sisera lay dead.

When the songs of Deborah were sung, one segment gave praise to the judge of Israel Deborah for the courage to arise and inspire men to arise and fight; subsequently, when honour will be given again, it will be towards Jael, where she was described as being the most blessed of women. The honour roll missed out on the very commander who led the troops out to battle. Leaders must always be discerning to not miss destiny-changing moments, and like in the story of Barak, be constantly reminded that honour flows towards those who take bold action.

- 💎 65 -

NEVER BELITTLE YOURSELF

"The angel of the Lord came and sat down under the oak in Ophrah that belonged to Joash the Abiezrite, where his son Gideon was threshing wheat in a winepress to keep it from the Midianites. When the angel of the Lord appeared to Gideon, he said, "The Lord is with you, mighty warrior."
—*Judges 6:11-12 NIV*

"They came up with their livestock and their tents like swarms of locusts. It was impossible to count them or their camels; they invaded the land to ravage it. Midian so impoverished the Israelites that they cried out to the Lord for help."
—*Judges 6:5, 6, NIV*

Mirror mirror on the wall. A classic line from a children's fantasy story. Every time you stare at the mirror, what you may see is the accurate representation of your physical attributes; your face's distinct features are correct, but there is a leadership representation inside many individuals, and unfortunately, because they can't see it, they belittle themselves and rule out any possibility of leading others. A certain man from the weak clan in one of the smallest tribes of Israel was threshing wheat in a wine press to keep it from the Midianites, who had become a thorn in the flesh of Isreal, when an angelic visitor appeared after piercing the fabric of time and space, making a declaration that will startle its hearer, "Gideon the Lord is with you, mighty warrior. Now remember this was a man hiding in a big hole in the ground; he would go on to have a verbal contest of his inadequacy, and the lord said, Go in the strength you have and assured him of his presence.

You must understand that God viewed him for who he really was and not who he thought he was. This same weak man would first destroy the altar of his father's house. Next, when the Midiannites, Amalekites, and other eastern people joined forces, when the spirit of the Lord came on him, he blew a trumpet that attracted thousands. Gideon, with the help of God, would use three hundred men to defeat this congregation of evil that was innumerable and were like locusts in the valley. When he pursued Zebah and Zalmunna, he did not hesitate to step forward and kill them, taking the ornaments off their camels. At this point a call was made to establish a kingship lineage in his family, and while he declined, it never eradicated who the leader of Israel was in his lifetime.

Have you lived a life of second guessing your leadership ability? Have you belittled your potential? Godly leaders understand this gem reminds them that all that is inside, is far greater than what is on the outside, and to never belittle the great impact your leadership can bring.

- 💎 66 -

AVOID EXCUSES

"The Lord turned to him and said, "Go in the strength you have and save Israel out of Midian's hand. Am I not sending you?" "Pardon me, my Lord," Gideon replied, "but how can I save Israel? My clan is the weakest in Manasseh, and I am the least in my family." The Lord answered, "I will be with you, and you will strike down all the Midianites, leaving none alive."
—*Judges 6:14-16, NIV*

In the earlier gem, we saw the rise of Gideon, and one trait he initially exhibited was giving excuses when the leadership call came. Gideon was quick to highlight the smallness and incapacitated nature of his background; he felt at a disadvantage and gave layers of excuses. His clan was small, and amongst the commonwealth of the sons of Jacob, the tribe of Manasseh was also not like that of the much bigger tribes, all excuses in the face of God. Godly leaders avoid excuses when called upon to act.

First, they must understand that who God calls, he also goes on to empower for the task ahead. Second, everyone possesses some form of handicap, whether obvious or not; therefore, what you may perceive as an advantage some other person has over you may be nothing more than an individual who has chosen to avoid excuses and deliver on his leadership mandateThe key is that leaders don't justify their actions; instead, they take the necessary actions.

- 💎 67 -

DETACH FROM THE PAST

"That same night the Lord said to him, "Take the second bull from your father's herd, the one seven years old. Tear down your father's altar to Baal and cut down the Asherah pole beside it. Then build a proper kind of altar to the Lord your God on the top of this height. Using the wood of the Asherah pole that you cut down, offer the second bull as a burnt offering."
—Judges 6:25-26, NIV

God making a call for Gideon to ascend to leadership made a demand of him to cut off from his idolatrous past; he was instructed to take a bull and tear down the altar to ball and cut down the Asherah pole beside it and build a proper altar to God. Gideon was afraid of his family and kinsmen. Infact choosing to carry out the instruction in the dead of the night. True to his thoughts, there was anger, and it led to his father defending him, asking why Baal would not fight for himself.

In the leadership story of many, there always lies a chapter when they had to detach from their past in order to move forward. The past possesses a seductive pull that can hamper the progress of a leader sometimes both spiritually and physically. The gem is that godly leaders must take out the much needed housekeeping in order to establish certain areas of the past that cannot accompany them into the future. Some of these have contained in them destructive elements that are prepared to make a mockery of their leadership call. Hold this principle close to your heart and keep meditating on what you must detach from; sometimes it could even be people. The mandate is much bigger than what people think of you, like in the case of Gideon.

- 💎 68 -

CLARION CALL

> *"Then the Spirit of the Lord came on Gideon, and he blew a trumpet, summoning the Abiezrites to follow him. He sent messengers throughout Manasseh, calling them to arms, and also into Asher, Zebulun and Naphtali, so that they too went up to meet them."*
> *—Judges 6:34,35, NIV*

A clarion call is a strongly expressed demand or request for action, and it is one that a leader will at one point of the other make while traversing their leadership journey. Gideon needed men to fight against the Midianites, and when the spirit of the Lord came upon him, he blew a trumpet to attract men, even sending messengers throughout his own tribe of Manasseh and also that of Asher, Zebulun, and Naphtali.

A godly leader must understand that an occasion may unravel that will lead you to make a clarion call, and one must not shrink away from that responsibility regardless of how overwhelming and terrifying the prospects of such an action are. You may have to blow a trumpet, maybe for assistance in a project or an initiative, or maybe to drum up support for an agenda dear to your heart. Mastering the art of making such an important call can be instrumental to your leadership success in ways you cannot imagine. The gem is to be prepared for such an inevitable task that will be the responsibility of anyone called to lead.

- 💎 69 -

NOT BY NUMBERS

"But the Lord said to Gideon, "There are still too many men. Take them down to the water, and I will thin them out for you there. If I say, 'This one shall go with you,' he shall go; but if I say, 'This one shall not go with you,' he shall not go." So Gideon took the men down to the water. There the Lord told him, "Separate those who lap the water with their tongues as a dog laps from those who kneel down to drink." Three hundred of them drank from cupped hands, lapping like dogs. All the rest got down on their knees to drink. The Lord said to Gideon, "With the three hundred men that lapped I will save you and give the Midianites into your hands. Let all the others go home." So Gideon sent the rest of the Israelites home but kept the three hundred, who took over the provisions and trumpets of the others. Now the camp of Midian lay below him in the valley."
—Judges 7:4-8, NIV

It's human nature to conclude that a leader with more men is sure to trump another with fewer followers, but one thing you must understand is that it is not only the majority but the quality of those following; this is further cemented when it is powered by the eternal excellency of the almighty. Gideon had issued a clarion call, to which many responded. However, one can only imagine the tension he must have experienced when God informed him that he had too many men, and that Midian would not be delivered to him due to potential pride and boasting of his soldiers.

He then led the remaining twenty-two thousand to a stream, where God instructed him to separate those who drank from those who knelt, leaving only three hundred men to face an impossible battle. With the spiritual strategies employed, the three hundred men should go on to defeat all their enemies. What is instructive is that God communicated a message that he doesn't need numbers; in fact, running through the pages of the Bible, you will find several accounts of a few taking on the majority because it is not by numbers.

As a God-fearing leader, you must resist the temptation to place your trust in the numbers you lead or command, lest you believe it is your acumen and intelligence quotient that saved the day, forgetting who truly gives a man victory in the world of men. The lesson here is unmistakable: don't rely solely on numbers; a select few, guided by the Lord, have the power to transform the world.

- 💎 70 -

DRAW ENCOURAGEMENT

"During that night the Lord said to Gideon, "Get up, go down against the camp, because I am going to give it into your hands. If you are afraid to attack, go down to the camp with your servant Purah and listen to what they are saying. Afterward, you will be encouraged to attack the camp." So he and Purah his servant went down to the outposts of the camp."
—*Judges 7:9-11, NIV*

Despite the title bestowed upon him by the angel of the Lord during the encounter, his miraculous disappearance into the flame, and the evidence of God's election of him as leader, Gideon was filled with fear. This fear was compounded by the fact that God had reduced his army from twenty-two thousand to just three hundred, and an imminent showdown loomed. Like most leaders, Gideon sought encouragement, and God recognized the crucial role it played in boosting his morale. During the night, he overheard a man discussing a dream with his friend, which his colleague interpreted as a sign that God had granted victory to the Midianites and their entire camp. This encouragement was all he needed to hear, and he returned to the camp, reassuring his men of their victory. The rest, as they say, is history; he and his band of three hundred will do the impossible; surely the encouragement of a vitamin boost does a lot for a leader.

Dear leader, do not underestimate the power surge that encouragement can provide to you and your team. As you strive to learn how to draw encouragement from various sources, it serves as a vital fuel that can propel your leadership vehicle to its destination. Ignoring it could jeopardize your leadership dream, especially since there is a high likelihood of experiencing fear, anxiety, or burnout. The key is to always have your internal tank filled with encouragement; you will be glad you did.

- 💎 71 -

LEAD BY EXAMPLE

"Watch me," he told them. "Follow my lead. When I get to the edge of the camp, do exactly as I do. When I and all who are with me blow our trumpets, then from all around the camp blow yours and shout, 'For the Lord and for Gideon."
—Judges 7:17, 18, NIV

I absolutely obsess over leaders who live by example; Jesus, for one, exemplified this with His life, showing the way and walking His talk, but many years before that, the leader Gideon showed that this was a medal he had pinned on his chest by leading from the front. Upon arriving at the Midinate camp, he divided the three hundred men into three companies, placing trumpets and empty jars with torches inside. His next words should serve as a mantra for every godly leader: "Watch me," "follow my lead." If all leaders adhered to this creed, society might have been better off, which is why Christ took on human form to demonstrate to his church the standards expected of leaders.

Unfortunately, we live in a time in human history where many leaders instead practice the creed: do what I say, but don't do what I do. In order to garner the admiration, respect, and loyalty of men, a leader must demonstrate leadership by taking the initiative. Nothing inspires men to take significant action and make unquantifiable sacrifices more than witnessing their leader walk the walk and not hide in the comfort of their position. The gem here is that godly leaders must always learn to lead by example. All of God's chosen vessels through scriptures were living examples of what they preached and expected of others; if you want people to act in a particular manner or act according to a particular code of conduct, lead by example.

- 💎 72 -

TACKLING RESENTMENT WITH EQ

"Now the Ephraimites asked Gideon, "Why have you treated us like this? Why didn't you call us when you went to fight Midian?" And they challenged him vigorously. But he answered them, "What have I accomplished compared to you? Aren't the gleanings of Ephraim's grapes better than the full grape harvest of Abiezer? God gave Oreb and Zeeb, the Midianite leaders, into your hands. What was I able to do compared to you?" At this, their resentment against him subsided."
—*Judges 8:1-3, NIV*

Remember our earlier short tale about Gideon's clarion call for men and the response of a few tribes? Well, one tribe felt slighted and showed their resentment by vigorously challenging him. The Ephraimites, instead of celebrating the great victory, asked why they were treated that way. In their view, they felt used, thinking maybe he was trying to keep them from sharing the spoils of war. Instead of recounting the supernatural instructions, he instead employed the use of emotional intelligence to tackle the resentment, showing himself to be diplomatic and understanding how a soft word can soften anger. He employed flattery and distraction by praising their roles, making them feel like the real victors, and highlighting their perceived importance.

He was able to ease the tension, causing the resentment to subside. As a godly leader, there will always be resentment by an individual or group of persons who genuinely believe they deserve more. The inability of any leader to tackle this level of resentment with EQ many determines the number of days such a leader may lead. Many who could have lasted long periods had their tenure short lived due to the lack of diplomacy in tackling resentment. The gem here is to learn and imbibe a culture of utilizing EQ to deal with human elements, which are a constant in the mathematical equation of any leadership journey.

- 💎 73 -

WARY OF DANGEROUS ENDORSEMENT

"The Israelites said to Gideon, "Rule over us—you, your son and your grandson—because you have saved us from the hand of Midian." But Gideon told them, "I will not rule over you, nor will my son rule over you. The Lord will rule over you."
—Judges 8:22, 23, NIV

Is it not surprising that after winning such a huge battle that a man would turn down a coronation and all the trappings that come with it, well that's just what Gideon did. After the conquest the Israelites said to him rule over us, lets establish a kingship lineage with you but to their utter shock he announced that he would not rule, nor would his son, rather the Lord will rule. In this era of Judges, before a kingship line was kickstarted by Saul, it was God's intent and his eternal plan that he will rule over His people. Gideon understood this and was wary of this seemingly harmless but very dangerous endorsement.

On the leadership ladder, most leaders will be confronted by this from men, and wise ones must be discerning enough to know what to accept and what to reject as it can sabotage or even destroy any leader who treats this gem with a pinch of salt. Everywhere and every time always lead in the consciousness of where power truly resides, whether its attributing to God all that is his, or honoring men who hold influence and sway over affairs, never try to exalt yourself. While such endorsements may appear harmless of any negative intent, it has the tendency to do much damage, Gideon knew though he was a leader he was not anointed to be king over Israel and rejected the endorsement.

How many godly leaders operating today have the humility to reject what many will give their lives for? If you truly want to excel, be cautious of dangerous premature endorsement, remember promotion comes neither from the east or the west, nor the south. But God is the judge who puts one down and sets another up. Be wise and stay wary of dangerous endorsements.

- 💎 74 -

WARY THAT YOUR ACTIONS DON'T ENSNARE

"Gideon made the gold into an ephod, which he placed in Ophrah, his town. All Israel prostituted themselves by worshiping it there, and it became a snare to Gideon and his family."
—Judges 8:27, NIV

Leaders must handle the following gem with the uptmost wisdom and maturity it deserves, otherwise what may be sincere actions can further ensnare others. Humans have a tendency to make doctrine out of the personal dealings of others and leaders are not exempt, and this leads to a society of individuals walking the highway of error. Gideon's first action was the total decimation of the idol of Baal in his fathers house and the evil Asherah ple beside it was cut down. But after the victory over Zebah and Zalmunna, and turning down the kingship, he requested a earring each from the plunder, which was placed on a garment and weighed about seventeen hundred shekels, mot counting the ornaments and pendants.

He would proceed to have the gold made into an ephod, which was a type of apron worn by the high priest and placed it his town Opharh and all Israel prostituted themselves by worshipping it there and it became a snare to Gideon and his family. He has done something wrong that led the people back to idolatry, though scripture does not explain his exact motivation, whether to seek guidance from God or other deities. As a leader he conveniently forgot that his influence, which leaders boast of, have the capacity to turn a religious icon into an object of worship. It is on record that he is the only judge who led Isreal down the path of infamy and must have brought great reproach and potential strife into his own household. Godly leaders must constantly have a caution light blinking on their mental dashboard not to take actions that have the propensity to lead people away from God.

- 💎 75 -

DANGER OF "LEADERSHIP BY ALL MEANS"

"Abimelek son of Jerub-Baal went to his mother's brothers in Shechem and said to them and to all his mother's clan, "Ask all the citizens of Shechem, 'Which is better for you: to have all seventy of Jerub-Baal's sons rule over you, or just one man?' Remember, I am your flesh and blood." When the brothers repeated all this to the citizens of Shechem, they were inclined to follow Abimelek, for they said, "He is related to us." They gave him seventy shekels of silver from the temple of Baal-Berith, and Abimelek used it to hire reckless scoundrels, who became his followers. He went to his father's home in Ophrah and on one stone murdered his seventy brothers, the sons of Jerub-Baal. But Jotham, the youngest son of Jerub-Baal, escaped by hiding. Then all the citizens of Shechem and Beth Millo gathered beside the great tree at the pillar in Shechem to crown Abimelek king. When Jotham was told about this, he climbed up on the top of Mount Gerizim and shouted to them, "Listen to me, citizens of Shechem, so that God may listen to you. One day the trees went out to anoint a king for themselves. They said to the olive tree, 'Be our king.' "But the olive tree answered, 'Should I give up my oil, by which both gods and humans are honored, to hold sway over the trees?' "Next, the trees said to the fig tree, 'Come and be our king.' "But the fig tree replied, 'Should I give up my fruit, so good and sweet, to hold sway over the trees?' "Then the trees said to the vine, 'Come and be our king.' "But the vine answered, 'Should I give

up my wine, which cheers both gods and humans, to
hold sway over the trees?' "Finally all the trees said to
the thornbush, 'Come and be our king.' "The thorn-
bush said to the trees, 'If you really want to anoint
me king over you, come and take refuge in my shade;
but if not, then let fire come out of the thornbush and
consume the cedars of Lebanon!"
—Judges 9:1-15, NIV

There is hardly any individual more dangerous than a man who is desperate for power, which means it portends great danger for all who are involved in ways that its ramifications cannot be easily measured. Abimelek was a son of Jerub-Baal (another name ascribed to Gideon); he was the son of a concubine; he applauded his kin's men and stirred an evil thought on why the people should have all of seventy of Gideon's sons ruling over them; when he alone could be leader, he reminded them of the bond of blood, requesting silver to hire mercenaries for his nefarious task. He went to his father's house and, on one stone, murdered his seventy brothers, with only the youngest escaping. On the day of his coronation, the only surviving brother Jotham stood on the Mount and gave a figurative expression of the drama playing out.

The trees approached the bramble, a thorny bush that lacks the same valuable attributes as the olive tree, the fig tree, and the vine. The bramble, unworthy of being a king, accepts the role despite its inadequacy. However, it cunningly uses its position to demand the loyalty of the other trees and threatens them with destruction if they refuse. This parable points to the importance of discerning leadership qualities and the dangers of seeking leadership for the wrong reasons. Just as the trees represented different candidates, we often encounter various individuals aspiring to leadership roles in various areas of life. Some may be genuinely motivated by a desire to serve and bless others, while others may be driven by self-interest and ambition.

The parable highlights the significance of humility and self-awareness in leadership. The olive tree, fig tree, and vine demonstrate humility by acknowledging their unique roles and recognizing that their contributions are meaningful in their own right. They choose not to forsake their callings for the pursuit of greater power.

On the other hand, the bramble's acceptance of the kingship represents a dangerous form of leadership that lacks substance, integrity, and genuine concern for others. The bramble's willingness to harm others to secure its position illustrates the destructive nature of selfish ambition in leadership. The gem here is that leaders must seek to examine the motive of why they want to lead; attempting to do otherwise never ends well, and Abimelek was no different, who, after going after the men in Mount Zalmon, set fire to the tower, leading to the deaths of about a thousand men and women.

His next attempt was at Thebez, and he besieged it and captured it. Inside the city, however, was a strong tower, to which all the men and women—all the people of the city—had fled. They had locked themselves in and climbed up on the tower roof. A woman dropped an upper millstone on his head and cracked his skull. Hurriedly, he called to his armour-bearer, "Draw your sword and kill me, so that they can't say, 'A woman killed him.'" So his servant ran him through, and he died. When the Israelites saw that Abimelek was dead, they went home. Thus God repaid the wickedness that Abimelek had done to his father by murdering his seventy brothers. God also made the people of Shechem pay for all their wickedness. The curse of Jotham son of Jerub-Baal came on them. A befitting end to a dangerous leader who wanted power by all means.

- 💎 76 -

CONSECRATION

"You will become pregnant and have a son whose head is never to be touched by a razor because the boy is to be a Nazirite, dedicated to God from the womb. He will take the lead in delivering Israel from the hands of the Philistines." But he said to me, 'You will become pregnant and have a son. Now then, drink no wine or other fermented drink and do not eat anything unclean, because the boy will be a Nazirite of God from the womb until the day of his death.' " So Manoah asked him, "When your words are fulfilled, what is to be the rule that governs the boy's life and work?"
—*Judges 13:5, 7, 12, NIV*

One of the most mind tasking questions I have ever been asked was by a wonderful lady, Adesewa Greg Ighodaro of the Corprate Church in Lagos, Nigeria. During our first interaction on working with my expressions, she asked a poignant question about my level of consecration for the leadership position I occupied. She would school me on how important it is for godly leaders to understand and daily be conscious of the consecration they must practice to lead effectively.

A certain man named Manoah had a wife who was childless, and an angel appeared to her and gave heaven's verdict that she would have a child. What stood out in this encounter was that the angel was quick to give the mother the consecration the unborn child must abide by to lead the Israelites; he was not to drink wine or any fermented drink, eat any unclean thing, and a razor was never to touch his head. God established for this new Judge of Isreal a personalized code of conduct that will be the barriers to avoid him falling off the edge of his journey. The manufacturer of your life knows your advantages and knows your potential weak points, and to address this is the consecration angle. The Consecration is in place for any godly leader who subscribes to God's way of leading; every leader must press into God, preferably before they embark on their journey, in order to know what the blueprint of the journey is and the consecration that will be the chaperone in their leadership.

- 💎 77 -

YOUR ACHILLES HEEL

"Then Samson's wife threw herself on him, sobbing, "You hate me! You don't really love me. You've given my people a riddle, but you haven't told me the answer." "I haven't even explained it to my father or mother," he replied, "so why should I explain it to you?" She cried the whole seven days of the feast. So on the seventh day he finally told her, because she continued to press him. She in turn explained the riddle to her people."
— Judges 14:16, 17, NIV

"Some time later, he fell in love with a woman in the Valley of Sorek whose name was Delilah. The rulers of the Philistines went to her and said, "See if you can lure him into showing you the secret of his great strength and how we can overpower him so we may tie him up and subdue him. Each one of us will give you eleven hundred shekels of silver."
— Judges 16:4,5, NIV

Every man has an Achilles's heel, a sort of weakness despite the overall strength that an individual possesses that can lead to a disastrous downfall. This idiomatic reference points to potential bobby traps in the life of a man and is spot on in the case of the strongest (physically) judge Israel ever had. Samson was picked for great things, but he had one major problem: women. Samson had a weakness not just for women but strange women and those of easy virtue. At one point in his quest for a Philistine wife, his parents asked if there was not an acceptable woman among his own people.

His first attempt at marriage led to chaos after he was cheated in a riddle competition by members of his wife's people (which God would use to stir up his anger and vengeance on the Philistines); this will lead to him setting their grain on fire with three hundred foxes, with torches on their tails. Like every weakness not acknowledged or tackled by its owner, it comes back rearing its head. Another woman would come into the life of Samson by the name Delilah, whom the rulers of Philistine approached and bribed with eleven hundred shekels of silver. She will go on and pester him for the secret of his superhuman strength, and he would on different occasions give false answers, and the woman would make a call that his enemies were upon him and he would rise and she would get upset.

Clearly, his weakness was so evident he didn't realize that his head lay on the laps of his enemy. With the number of false alarms, the Bible said she nagged him until he was sick to death of it and gave up the secrets of his strength, declaring that no razor had ever been used on him since birth and shaving him, he would become as weak as any other man. After putting him to sleep, she got someone to shave it all and called for the Philistines, who seized him, gouged his eyes out, and bound him with bronze shackles, and he was set to grind grain in the prison—a disappointing end of a leader.

Though God honored him in death by causing him to kill more Philistines in death than in life, the gem is that every godly leader must identify the inherent weak spots and do all necessary to ensure that it doesn't lead to his or her downfall. Self-awareness and necessary action are the antidotes to any Achilles heel.

- 💎 78 -

LEADERS MUST KEEP VITAL INFORMATION SECRET

"When Delilah saw that he had told her everything, she sent word to the rulers of the Philistines, "Come back once more; he has told me everything." So the rulers of the Philistines returned with the silver in their hands."
—*Judges 16:18, NIV*

In the world of leaders, there is always someone looking forward to their downfall. It doesn't matter how good, capable, or anointed they are; whether they eradicate poverty, heal the sick, or discover the cure for cancer, there will always be one person who will seek to pay any price to see that leader fall or fail.

In the case of Samson, due to his inability to keep vital information, he forgot that for those without God, there is always a price to buy them over. He gave away the source of his power to a woman who looked forward to a payout on his very life. As a godly leader, walk in the consciousness that vital areas of your life must be kept off limits no matter the temptation.

Leaders must install guard rails or gatekeepers over their mouth, whose responsibility is to ensure that leaders don't release information that can be detrimental when it becomes public knowledge, therefore such information must never escape into the ears of those who seek to profit from owning such secrets.

The gem here is that smart, godly leaders never share everything about themselves, their operations, and their affairs with those closest to them; they walk in wisdom by retaining some vital pieces for themselves. Never be so trusting to give the entire gamut of your life to another mortal; it may very well be used against you.

- 💎 79 -

NEVER FOR HIRE

"A young Levite from Bethlehem in Judah, who had been living within the clan of Judah, left that town in search of some other place to stay. On his way he came to Micah's house in the hill country of Ephraim. Then Micah said to him, "Live with me and be my father and priest, and I'll give you ten shekels of silver a year, your clothes and your food." So the Levite agreed to live with him, and the young man became like one of his sons to him. Then Micah installed the Levite, and the young man became his priest and lived in his house. And Micah said, "Now I know that the Lord will be good to me, since this Levite has become my priest."
—Judges 17:7-8, 10-13, NIV

"He told them what Micah had done for him, and said, "He has hired me and I am his priest."
—Judges 18:4, NIV

"They answered him, "Be quiet! Don't say a word. Come with us, and be our father and priest. Isn't it better that you serve a tribe and clan in Israel as priest rather than just one man's household?" The priest was very pleased. He took the ephod, the household gods and the idol and went along with the people."
—Judges 18:19, 20, NIV

A leader must never be for hire; there must never be a convenient price tag for your service to others. Once this becomes a reality, you lose the very core virtue of leadership, which is respect. A young Levite from Bethlehem left his town in search of some other place. A consecrated priest to God who clearly understood his mandate. He would encounter a man called Micah who offered free accommodation and food in exchange for serving as his personal priest.

This same man was offered a bigger offer by some Danites, who gave him an opportunity to be the priest of their clan and use the idol from his previous employer. While there is no mention of any negative outcome for this leader, it is imperative that godly leaders must never be at the beck and call for the highest bidder; your loyalty is first to God and those you are truly called to serve.

- 💎 80 -

LEADERS ARE IMPORTANT

"In those days Israel had no king; everyone did as they saw fit."
—*Judges 21:25, NIV*

The importance of a leader is one people tend to underestimate, but any godly leader must carry the remembrance that their role is a scared one. The absence of leadership means the presence of things that words may do great injustice to summarize. It is said that in those days that Israel had no king, and everyone did as they saw fit. We can both jointly go on a mental excursion to imagine the decay, the debauched behavior of the people in the absence of law and order, and a leader to see to its enforcement.

The corruption was rife; we can see great idolatry in the Northern part of the kingdom with the tribe of Dan standing out or immorality in the South, with the tribe of Benjamin championing that narrative. This gem is a reminder that leaders are needed and important for balance. Never buy into the agenda that you are a spare to society; you are the glue that keeps things together. As such, you must never let those you lead and yourself down; your absence means chaos. You, my friend, are important.

THE BOOK OF
RUTH

- 81 -

GENEROSITY

"Boaz asked the overseer of his harvesters, "Who does that young woman belong to?" So Boaz said to Ruth, "My daughter, listen to me. Don't go and glean in another field and don't go away from here. Stay here with the women who work for me."
—Ruth 2:5, 8, NIV

"The Lord bless him!" Naomi said to her daughter-in-law. "He has not stopped showing his kindness to the living and the dead." She added, "That man is our close relative; he is one of our guardian-redeemers."
—Ruth 2:20, NIV

In the book of Ruth, the star character by all accounts is Ruth the Moabite, who accompanied her mother-in-law Naomi after the loss of her husband to Bethlehem, where she did menial work. But for the purpose of this gem, I believe that one leader stands out in the story who showed such generosity that may have further cemented in the lineage of David, the future King of Israel, showing generosity to someone who clearly couldn't repay anything back and even further down, marrying her to maintain the name of the dead with his property.

By this generous purchase, he ensured he saved both Naomi and Ruth. His action mirrored what Jesus Christ will do years later, saving us when we were nothing and had nothing, purchasing us with his blood so we can have a lineage with him. Leaders must learn to show generosity. I very much doubt Boaz thought further down the line of the ramifications of his action; he only expressed what was already part of his character, which was generosity.

Godly leaders never fail to show acts of generosity towards all those who come their way and most especially to those who have nothing to give back. The gem is, dear leader, be generous; men honor generosity, and God blesses generosity.

THE BOOK OF
I SAMUEL

- 💎 82 -

LEADER AND FAMILY PROBLEMS

"Wherefore the sin of the young men was very great before the LORD: for men abhorred the offering of the LORD."
—I Samuel 2:17, KJV

"Now Eli, who was very old, heard about everything his sons were doing to all Israel and how they slept with the women who served at the entrance to the tent of meeting. So he said to them, "Why do you do such things? I hear from all the people about these wicked deeds of yours. No, my sons; the report I hear spreading among the Lord's people is not good. The time is coming when I will cut short your strength and the strength of your priestly house, so that no one in it will reach old age, and you will see distress in my dwelling. Although good will be done to Israel, no one in your family line will ever reach old age. " 'And what happens to your two sons, Hophni and Phinehas, will be a sign to you—they will both die on the same day. I will raise up for myself a faithful priest, who will do according to what is in my heart and mind. I will firmly establish his priestly house, and they will minister before my anointed one always."
—I Samuel 2:22-35, KJV

"In that day I will perform against Eli all things which I have spoken concerning his house: when I begin, I will also make an end. For I have told him that I will judge his house for ever for the iniquity which he knoweth; because his sons made themselves

vile, and he restrained them not. And therefore I have swore unto the house of Eli, that the iniquity of Eli's house shall not be purged with sacrifice nor offering for ever."
—*I Samuel 3:12-14, KJV*

"The name of his firstborn was Joel and the name of his second was Abijah, and they served at Beersheba. But his sons did not follow his ways. They turned aside after dishonest gain and accepted bribes and perverted justice."
—*I Samuel 8:2, 3, KJV*

Nothing is more troubling for leaders than domestic problems. While it seems you are the captain of the world on one hand, on the other you are struggling to stay afloat, whether it's with spouses, children, or relatives. Nothing will stretch the emotional bandwidth of a leader more than problems at home, and any leader who is unable to walk safely at what may be termed a potential landmine may struggle in their leadership of others.

Whether it is familiarity, leaders from every walk of life, from the church to politics to the community, exude so much confidence but shy away in embarrassment at the antics of those closest to them; therefore, this gem must not be swept under the carpet. Eli was the priest at the time, and he heard everything his sons, Hophni and Phinehas were doing, from selecting the best portions of the offerings to committing immorality at the entrance of the hallowed tent of the meeting, and even though he made mention to them of their evil ways, it is evident he did not take any drastic act to stem the tide, leading God to issue through his successor Samuel punishments that, in the wisdom of God, were in sync with their years of sin. No one was to reach old age in the house of Eli, the prophecy of the death of Hophni and Phinehas, who after growing up in the temple should know better than anyone else, and that the iniquity of Eli's house shall not be purged with sacrifice and offering forever.

As the story goes, God's words came to pass, and upon hearing the terrible news of his sons who went into battle with the philistines passing away, and the Ark of God lost to Isreal's enemy, Eli fell backwards and broke his neck instantly dying after leading the nation for forty years. Even his successor in ministry and leadership of Israel, Samuel, also had a fair share of domestic troubles. In old age, he appointed his sons, Joel and Abijah to rule, but they did not follow his ways, turned aside after dishonest gain, and accepted bribes and perverted justice, leading to an outcry from the elders of Israel.

The two scenarios painted must have caused great pain to the leaders Eli and Samuel and call for closer introspection on how leaders should manage their domestic affairs before it destroys not just their leadership or legacy but their very lives. Everyone is bound to have his own fair share—kids of a pastor not interested in God, wards of a political leader who commits all sorts of vices, but only let off the hook because of the connection of their parents. Godly leaders must handle this sensitive matter with the combination of prayer, emotional intelligence, and positive and quick action (not just mere words like Eli).

A leader's first ministry is his family. He or she must thus ensure it is treated with the same level of discipline mixed with love; the real success of leadership is that of the home.

- 💎 83 -

LEARN TO TURN ASIDE QUICKLY WHEN TREADING A DANGEROUS PATH

"Why do you harden your hearts as the Egyptians and Pharaoh did? When Israel's god dealt harshly with them, did they not send the Israelites out so they could go on their way?"
—I Samuel 6:6, NIV

It's surprising that our next gem comes from the priests and diviners of Philistine. The ark of God had been with them for seven months, and they had suffered great loss from the image of Dagon, their god, bowing to the ark, to devastation and afflictions of tumor on the people, followed by death and panic, raising an outcry that reached heaven.

The spiritual leaders of the people advised the political leaders of certain acts to take, including making gold tumors and gold rats and sending the ark back into Israelite territory, but the stand out verse for me was how they realized their hearers were harden like the Egyptians and how God dealt with them accordingly, their immediate act of repentance after realizing it was a dangerous path for the nation.

As a godly leader, you must ensure that you never carry the heart posture of the Egyptians, who, in the face of total destruction and death, hardened their hearts until imminent death in the Red Sea. Godly leaders turn aside quickly and retrace their steps from erroneous paths to avoid disastrous consequences; don't let hubris destroy your leadership; always listen out for the voice of wisdom around you; in the case of the Philstines, it was their priests and diviners.

- 💎 84 -

LEADERS MUST KEEP VITAL INFORMATION SECRET

"Then Samuel said, "Assemble all Israel at Mizpah, and I will intercede with the Lord for you." When they had assembled at Mizpah, they drew water and poured it out before the Lord. On that day they fasted and there they confessed, "We have sinned against the Lord." Now Samuel was serving as leader of Israel at Mizpah. They said to Samuel, "Do not stop crying out to the Lord our God for us, that he may rescue us from the hand of the Philistines."
—I Samuel 7:5-6, 8, NIV

There is a responsibility that most leaders abdicate, and that is exercising spiritual authority and making intercessions for those given to them to lead. Though not expressly stated in many job descriptions of leaders, it is clearly an obvious one that must be exercised. Samuel had asked that all Israel assemble at Mizpah, and he would intercede on their behalf against the Philistines, and his prayers would aid Israel. When their enemies heard, they had assembled to fight them, God roared with thunder, throwing them into panic.

Thereafter, Samuel set up the famous stone called Ebenezer and completely silenced the Philistine's continuous embarrassment. I believe strongly that as godly leaders it behooves on us to exercise authority on our knees; there can only be positive outcomes from such an act. The gem here is not to be carried away only by the seen but to spend equal time on the unseen; you are also called to spiritual authority.

- 💎 85 -

WHAT WILL BE YOUR CLAIM?

"Samuel told all the words of the Lord to the people who were asking him for a king. He said, "This is what the king who will reign over you will claim as his rights: He will take your sons and make them serve with his chariots and horses, and they will run in front of his chariots. Some he will assign to be commanders of thousands and commanders of fifties, and others to plow his ground and reap his harvest, and still others to make weapons of war and equipment for his chariots. He will take your daughters to be perfumers and cooks and bakers. He will take the best of your fields and vineyards and olive groves and give them to his attendants. He will take a tenth of your grain and of your vintage and give it to his officials and attendants. Your male and female servants and the best of your cattle and donkeys he will take for his own use. He will take a tenth of your flocks, and you yourselves will become his slaves. But the people refused to listen to Samuel. "No!" they said. "We want a king over us. Then we will be like all the other nations, with a king to lead us and to go out before us and fight our battles."
— I Samuel 8:10-17, 19-20, NIV

The Israelites had envied their Canaanite neighbors for so long; walking into battle, they had seen the lone character probably dressed in separate battle attire, surrounded by royal bodyguards, with flags fluttering in the wind, and thousands of the Calvary waiting for the command of this one special man. Give us a king, they said to Samuel. The prophet would highlight to them some drawbacks due to what he described as excesses of a king. He reminded them that he would make some claims as rights, have servants to serve him, work for his food, make equipment, how he would have the best pick in terms of picking his women, eat the best of the land, and own so much more, but the people refused.

While there is nothing wrong in enjoying the perks of one's position, it's evident that many leaders are fulfilling Samuel's prophecy by staking huge claims due to their positions. Godly leaders understand one thing, power, like life, is transient, and they do their best not to define their leadership opportunity with any claiming rights. I know of leaders who chose not to take salaries. These breeds, I know, are far in between what you and I see in our world today, but never the less, it should not deter the rise of more leaders who align more with the people they lead, their needs, and their concerns, rather than their comfort and belly. The gem here is to be guided when daydreaming on what your claim would be; that is not the definition of leadership; rather, in one word, it is service.

- 💎 86 -

LEADERSHIP CAN COME FROM ANYWHERE

"Saul approached Samuel in the gateway and asked, "Would you please tell me where the seer's house is?" "I am the seer," Samuel replied. "Go up ahead of me to the high place, for today you are to eat with me, and in the morning I will send you on your way and will tell you all that is in your heart. As for the donkeys you lost three days ago, do not worry about them; they have been found. And to whom is all the desire of Israel turned, if not to you and your whole family line?" Saul answered, "But am I not a Benjamite, from the smallest tribe of Israel, and is not my clan the least of all the clans of the tribe of Benjamin? Why do you say such a thing to me?"
—I Samuel 9:18-21, NIV

Ever seen a rose grow out of a crack in the concrete? That must be the best metaphor to describe this gem that leadership can come from anywhere. Saul the Benjamite was handsome, described as a head taller than anyone else. His father's donkey got lost, and when hopeless, his servant recommended they seek out a seer in the town. Upon entering the town, they met Samuel, who instructed him to go to the high place to share a meal, where he unveiled God's plan for the young Saul, who was quick to echo his inadequacy, especially as regards his place of birth, clan, and tribe.

The truth is, leaders can come from about anywhere; there is no prescribed manual book that specifies the winepress where leaders are formed and made. Clearly, there were qualities that God saw in Saul despite his personal hesitation. Leaders must not be overtly fearful when the mantle falls on their laps, especially if the major restriction they have is self-imposed. The gem here is that your background does not dictate how well you can function and perform as a leader; therefore, erase any mental roadblocks and drive towards a life of leading for change.

- 💎 87 -

PREMATURE ANNOUNCEMENT

"Now Saul's uncle asked him and his servant, "Where have you been?" "Looking for the donkeys," he said. "But when we saw they were not to be found, we went to Samuel." Saul's uncle said, "Tell me what Samuel said to you." Saul replied, "He assured us that the donkeys had been found." But he did not tell his uncle what Samuel had said about the kingship."
—I Samuel 10:14-16, NIV

Whether out of fear of the scoundrels who would thunder, how can this fellow save us? Maybe that's why when Saul's uncle asked him and his servant where they had been, he was prudent not to mention anything about his kingship; after all, this should be a moment of great pride for his entire family. When applying wisdom to the things of life, you will realize that premature announcement of your leadership can be dangerous and lead to an abortion in some regard. You see, for every manifestation, there is a right season for the announcement. While my season will be much different from yours, it is important to stress that you must guard your ascension to the throne. Saul, beyond his personal limitations, also knew the resistance he may have from the people around him.

Your kingship, in my opinion, should not be a public announcement until the crown is sitting on your head. The gem here is to avoid the urge to prematurely announce your leadership rise, allow the stars to align, and let the time be right to reduce the opposition and, even more importantly, catch everyone unaware.

- ◈ 88 -

IT'S HUMAN TO BE FEARFUL

"When Samuel had all Israel come forward by tribes, the tribe of Benjamin was taken by lot. Then he brought forward the tribe of Benjamin, clan by clan, and Matri's clan was taken. Finally Saul son of Kish was taken. But when they looked for him, he was not to be found. So they inquired further of the Lord, "Has the man come here yet?" And the Lord said, "Yes, he has hidden himself among the supplies."
— I Samuel 10:20-22, NIV

Fear can be disastrous for any leader, but it is one that is present even inside the very best of us. It is human to be fearful. Saul had been handpicked to be the first King of Israel; he was to start a lineage of kings that would rule Israel forever, and when Samuel had all of Israel come forward by tribes and by lot, it fell on Benjamin and on Matri's clan and eventually on Saul the son of Kish, but there was one problem: the new king was nowhere to be found. The search party was out, but Samuel made an inquiry of the one whose eyes go to and fro the earth to ask the location of Saul, and it will surprise you that this tall and athletic choice had hidden himself among the supplies.

They ran and brought him out, declaring to all people to see the man the Lord had chosen with chants of, "Long live the King!" It is human to be fearful; leaders are allowed to feel fear and not feel negative or guilty about it. The gem is here whilst acknowledging this universal emotion is to ensure that such fear never paralyzes your leadership abilities. A godly leader must understand that the Lord has not given us a spirit of fear but of power, love, and a sound mind.

- 💎 89 -

RIGHTS AND DUTIES OF A LEADER

"Samuel explained to the people the rights and duties of kingship. He wrote them down on a scroll and deposited it before the Lord. Then Samuel dismissed the people to go to their own homes."
—*I Samuel 10:25, NIV*

Samuel, after presenting Saul, did something instructive; he knew the leader must not have a free rein to do whatever comes to his mind, which leads to dictatorship; instead, he explained to the people the rights and duties of kingship, writing them on a scroll and depositing it before the Lord. As a leader, are you aware of what your rights and duties that govern your role are, or do you just get by according to what the day presents? A godly leader must first be aware of his rights and duties and secondly must abide by them. The reason we find so many leaders making a mess of leadership opportunities, first starts from ignorance and/ or deciding not to follow through on set rules or laws . Wherever you find yourself, it is a duty you owe to yourself and to God to know your rights and duties.

- 💎 90 -

LOOK OUT FOR THE TURNING POINT

"Nahash the Ammonite went up and besieged Jabesh Gilead. And all the men of Jabesh said to him, "Make a treaty with us, and we will be subject to you." But Nahash the Ammonite replied, "I will make a treaty with you only on the condition that I gouge out the right eye of every one of you and so bring disgrace on all Israel." Just then Saul was returning from the fields, behind his oxen, and he asked, "What is wrong with everyone? Why are they weeping?" Then they repeated to him what the men of Jabesh had said. When Saul heard their words, the Spirit of God came powerfully upon him, and he burned with anger. They told the messengers who had come, "Say to the men of Jabesh Gilead, 'By the time the sun is hot tomorrow, you will be rescued.'" When the messengers went and reported this to the men of Jabesh, they were elated."
— I Samuel 11:1-2, 5-6, 9, NIV

There is always a fork in the road for every leader, a turning point that totally changes a leader's trajectory. In the case of Saul, it was triggered by the Ammonite called Nahash who besiege Jabesh, and when the people offered a treaty, he said he would only consider if he could gouge out the right eye of all the inhabitants. On seeing the people weep, the spirit of God came upon Saul, and he burned with anger, sending word back to the people of that region that they would be rescued from their enemies the next day. You must understand that all up to that point we had a newly anointed and crowned King who was struggling to win the hearts and minds of people who had never had a King before and only took the word of Prophet Samuel.

In leadership, it is imperative to win the people you intend to lead over, and this usually happens after a turning point, which, if you are sensitive and discerning enough to understand, is a golden ticket of your endorsement. Saul did just that and at night broke into the camp of the Ammonites and slaughtered them till afternoon the next day, so that those who survived were scattered. At this point his acceptance was complete, and he was truly their king; some even echoed, "Who was it that asked, shall Saul reign over us? Turn these men over to be killed." The entire people went to Gilgal and made Saul King in the presence of the Lord, followed by offerings and a great celebration. The gem is looking for the turning point; every leader will have a number of opportunities presented to them.

- 💎 91 -

TIMELESS INTEGRITY

"Samuel said to all Israel, "I have listened to every-thing you said to me and have set a king over you. Now you have a king as your leader. As for me, I am old and gray, and my sons are here with you. I have been your leader from my youth until this day. Here I stand. Testify against me in the presence of the Lord and his anointed. Whose ox have I taken? Whose donkey have I taken? Whom have I cheated? Whom have I oppressed? From whose hand have I accepted a bribe to make me shut my eyes? If I have done any of these things, I will make it right." "You have not cheated or oppressed us," they replied. "You have not taken anything from anyone's hand." Samuel said to them, "The Lord is witness against you, and also his anointed is witness this day, that you have not found anything in my hand." "He is witness," they said."
—I Samuel 12:1-5, NIV

So many things have the capability to outlive a man; very few have the capacity to inspire others long after. Integrity is timeless from the word integer, which means one of the same. Samuel displayed an unusually high level of integrity that is rare amongst leaders. At his old age, he said to Israel that he led from a young age and went on to reel his integrity credentials; he never took the ox or donkey of another man or cheated or oppressed or collected a bribe, asking that the Lord be his witness.

Godly leaders must understand that God is very big on the integrity of leaders because they echo through time like a pleasant sound that is pleasing to all who hear it, inspiring others to do more. Never be afraid to lead with integrity. What should guide you is that anything you do in private, you should have no apprehension if it was made into a movie and played on a large cinematic screen for the whole world to enjoy. Will you be applauded after the credits start rolling or be booed at for being a fraud? The gem here for godly leaders is integrity; it offers freedom to leaders who live by it to act without fear. Be a leader with integrity; she pays huge dividends to those who walk with her. As a godly leader, can you be trusted? Can you receive the same testimony as Samuel and be known for your honesty, reliability, and trustworthiness?

- 💎 92 -

AVOID IMPATIENCE

"When the Israelites saw that their situation was critical and that their army was hard pressed, they hid in caves and thickets, among the rocks, and in pits and cisterns. Some Hebrews even crossed the Jordan to the land of Gad and Gilead. Saul remained at Gilgal, and all the troops with him were quaking with fear. He waited seven days, the time set by Samuel; but Samuel did not come to Gilgal, and Saul's men began to scatter. So he said, "Bring me the burnt offering and the fellowship offerings." And Saul offered up the burnt offering. Just as he finished making the offering, Samuel arrived, and Saul went out to greet him. "What have you done?" asked Samuel. Saul replied, "When I saw that the men were scattering, and that you did not come at the set time, and that the Philistines were assembling at Mikmash..."
—I Samuel 13:6-11, NIV

Impatience from the time of Adam to the present day has caused men irreparable damages; the inability for leaders to trust God and put their complete faith in him has cost men the crowns on their heads, and Saul the first King of Israel was about to experience this. For understanding purposes, you must appreciate the fact that God is a supreme being who believes in order; he allocates responsibilities to men based on His superior wisdom and expects those sacred boundaries to be respected by all.

The office of a priest was distinct from that of the King, almost like our modern day separation of powers in government, i.e., the Legislature, Judiciary, and Executive. One party cannot annex the responsibilities of others; otherwise, the equilibrium of order would not only be disturbed, but stepping into another office for which you are not consecrated and called into may mean even death. The Israeli army was filled with fear; they were overwhelmed by the might of the enemies; many hid in holes and caves, quaking with fear. The prophet Samuel had mentioned he would be available to offer the burnt offerings to God, and I sincerely believe that God intentionally restrained him to test the heart of the leader of His people.

After seven days, Samuel was a no show, and Saul started to have deserters from his troops. Rather than trust God, his apprehension pushed him to impatience, causing him to temporarily forget his role and place in God's divine order. He called for the burnt offering and offered it, and just as he finished, guess who showed up? The very Prophet Smauel. How convenient. His first words to the King were, what have you done? His feeble reply was that he was more concerned about the feelings of men than those of the one who put him on the throne. There were grave consequences for his action, which would be visited shortly, but the gem for godly leaders is to understand the offspring of impatience is never truly a reflection of the outcome you desire; if you intend to lead, it must always be done with obedience and patience. This is not a call to leadership paralysis, but to ensure that you allow yourself to be prayerfully guided when pushed to the wall. It pays to be patient. A future king of Israel would declare that patience brings peace and, more importantly, better than pride, as pride leads to destruction. This was Saul's lot.

- 💎 93 -

BRAVERY

"But the men said to Saul, "Should Jonathan die—he who has brought about this great deliverance in Israel? Never! As surely as the Lord lives, not a hair of his head will fall to the ground, for he did this today with God's help." So the men rescued Jonathan, and he was not put to death."
— I Samuel 14:45, NIV

Jonathan, the son of Saul, was a special breed, especially with his relationship with David, who would succeed his father. What personally endears me to the young prince must in this instance be his bravery. He would make an audacious brave move, and the resultant effect of bravery amongst men is that people will rise to defend you. He called on his armor-bearer, asking that they go to the Philistine outpost without telling his father, saying perhaps the Lord will act on their behalf, and his loyal armor-bearer, captivated by the bravery, said his very heart and soul were intertwined with that of Jonathan.

He hatched a plan, and when he got the nudge that the Philistines who saw him would be delivered to him, he climbed up, and in the first attack, he and his armor-bearer killed some twenty men in a half-acre area. Panic struck the rest of the camp until victory was gained. Prior to this time, King Saul made a decree that his fighting men were under an oath not to eat, cursing anyone who did before evening. While marching, they saw honey on the ground, and Jonathan, who had not heard the decree, reached out his staff to taste it.

After another day of battle, Saul called for lots to be drawn for anyone in camp who had committed any sin when God did not answer his request, and Jonathan was pointed at. He confessed his deed to his father, who declared he would die, but men arose to defend the young prince.

Godly leaders must adopt a brave disposition in their affairs. The gem is to remember that bravery pays. People around you want to follow a brave leader and not a coward, and many will lay down everything to defend such an individual.

- 💎 94 -

HEAD HUNTING

"All the days of Saul there was bitter war with the Philistines, and whenever Saul saw a mighty or brave man, he took him into his service."
—I Samuel 14:52, NIV

Headhunters are a prominent feature in today's business world, professionals whose sole task is to connect talents to organizations that have people gaps. In leadership, it is important for leaders to also have the posture of head hunters. King Saul impressed in this regard; since all his days of rulership he was at war, he understood the importance of talent to get the better of the enemy, and whenever he saw a mighty or brave man, he would take him into service. A wise move, if I must say. You will always have areas of gap or areas that are in need of improvement when leading others; beyond service, you must constantly be on the lookout for those whose paths cross yours and who carry in many regards skills, talents, and the right mix of personality to make your job easier.

Each interaction must be seen as a potential interview to beef up your manpower needs. Godly leaders understand that what I am referencing here is competence. I have seen many Christians shy away from employing those who don't share their faith, conviction, or belong to their branch of Christianity. As a leader, you may be called to serve those of diverse orientations, creeds, and biases; therefore, the same way your team will deliver on your vision, their membership should be based on what they can bring to the table for you to be a success. The gem here, as we can see, is to make no room for discrimination. Leaders always seek to draft competent hands to ensure victory in their leadership battles.

- 💎 95 -

DISOBEDIENCE AND ARROGANCE

"Now go, attack the Amalekites and totally destroy all that belongs to them. Do not spare them; put to death men and women, children and infants, cattle and sheep, camels and donkeys. Then Saul attacked the Amalekites all the way from Havilah to Shur, near the eastern border of Egypt. He took Agag king of the Amalekites alive, and all his people he totally destroyed with the sword. But Saul and the army spared Agag and the best of the sheep and cattle, the fat calves and lambs—everything that was good. These they were unwilling to destroy completely, but everything that was despised and weak they totally destroyed. "I regret that I have made Saul king, because he has turned away from me and has not carried out my instructions." Samuel was angry, and he cried out to the Lord all that night. Early in the morning Samuel got up and went to meet Saul, but he was told, "Saul has gone to Carmel. There he has set up a monument in his own honor and has turned and gone on down to Gilgal." When Samuel reached him, Saul said, "The Lord bless you! I have carried out the Lord's instructions." But Samuel said, "What then is this bleating of sheep in my ears? What is this lowing of cattle that I hear?" But Samuel replied: "Does the Lord delight in burnt offerings and sacrifices as much as in obeying the Lord? To obey is better than sacrifice, and to heed is better than the fat of rams. For rebellion is like the sin of divination, and arrogance like the evil of

*idolatry. Because you have rejected the word of the
Lord, he has rejected you as king."*
—I Samuel 15:3, 7-9, 11-14, 22-23, NIV

Nothing has dragged down leaders from lofty heights more than disobedience and arrogance; all through the millennia, we see leaders who allowed acts of disobedience to soil their white apparel in the sight of God and to the disdain of men. God gave his chosen king Saul what was a simple and clear mission: go and attack the Amalekites and totally destroy all that belongs to them, men and women, children and infants, cattle and sheep, camels and donkeys. Instead he took into custody Agag King of the Amalekites alive and the best of the sheep and cattle, the fat calves and lambs—everything that was good. At that point the word of the Lord came to Samuel that God himself regretted making Saul King because he turned away from Him and did not obey instructions. Samuel cried all night, appealing to God. Early in the morning he made his way to Saul, and the first words he uttered were lies that he had carried out God's instruction, to which the angry prophet would reply if his ears were deceiving him. Hearing the bleating of sheep and mooing of the cattle, he went on to school him on the importance of obedience and how it's better than sacrifice. Reaching out to hold the prophet, he tore a part of his garment, and it was declared that the kingdom was torn away from him. Samuel put Agag to death himself.

The grave consequences of disobedience had reverberating effects across destinies. At that moment, the crown located and settled on a lowly shepherd boy. What is instructive to note is the comparison made: God equates rebellion with divination and arrogance with idolatry.

The gem here is that godly leaders must avoid all shades of disobedience and arrogance in leading others. God is particular about the hearts of men and listens to their cries with close attention; as such, he is very interested in the affairs of those called to shepherd others having hearts that are anchored to His ways. Arrogant and disobedient leaders always come to ruin; history backs this assertion.

- 💎 96 -

FEAR OF MEN

"Then Saul said to Samuel, "I have sinned. I violated the Lord's command and your instructions. I was afraid of the men and so I gave in to them."
—I Samuel 15:24, NIV

King Saul's feeble defense to Samuel's delivery of God's judgment was an acknowledgment that he had committed a sin by violating the Lord's command, and he gave his reason to be the fear of men. I know from my leadership journey how difficult it is when a leader is confronted with the voices of the multitude, a potpourri of views and opinions. Sometimes the volume levels can be so high and can deafen the leader, causing him to act contrary to what is right.

Saul had a choice, like most leaders will, to choose between pleasing God or pleasing men; each choice produces a starkly different outcome and consequence. The gem here is that godly leaders must never be intimidated by men that they put aside God's instructions; we must never allow the scary faces of men to cower us into making life-altering decisions that can end our lives or extinguish our leadership potentials. It is better to be hung out by men than to be deserted by God. If for a moment you think

the face of mortal men is scary, may you never have to see
the judgment face of the Creator; be obedient and humble;
follow God's instructions to the letter.

- 💎 97 -

HEART POSTURE

"When they arrived, Samuel saw Eliab and thought, "Surely the Lord's anointed stands here before the Lord." But the Lord said to Samuel, "Do not consider his appearance or his height, for I have rejected him. The Lord does not look at the things people look at. People look at the outward appearance, but the Lord looks at the heart."
—I Samuel 16:6, 7, NIV

The posture of the heart refers to both the position and equally important its condition. This is an internal X-ray of your innermost thoughts, desires, and motives—something that is totally impossible for another man except powered by the Holy Spirit to know. This is one of the things that makes God who he is; he dives straight into the deep end of the pool to search out things that cannot be easily sought out; like an archeologist, he unearths what lies beneath the surface, and with that, he makes his decisions. Saul had been rejected King, and it was only a matter of time that the spiritual declaration would find material expression in the earth realm. God instructed the prophet Samuel to seek out his new chosen vessel, and he arrived at the house of Jesse, a man who was blessed with eight sons. When the Prophet requested to see them, and when he saw Eliab, he was we convinced that he was the chosen one; after all he was head above shoulders and good looking, so he must be the one. after all, Saul was head above shoulders and good-looking, so he must be the one. But God corrected that wrong impression, saying that when it comes to leadership, it's not by height or appearance, and he had rejected the supposed choice of Israel's most powerful prophet; let's imagine God had not spoken to him and the dire consequences. God gave the prophet what he looks for, first stating that he does not look at what other men look at, which is the outward appearance, but he looks at the hearts of men. Which means God did an electrocardiogram on the heart, but instead of the physical activity, he searched the spiritual posture of the heart. In David, he saw the loving heart of a shepherd who could lead his people. The gem here is that godly leaders must constantly put the motives of their heart and its posture under God's microscope to ensure that they are always aligned and connected to his heart. Do not be carried away by outward things if you seek to lead, but invest time in ensuring your heart posture is right with God.

- 💎 98 -

LEADERS CARE

"Early in the morning David left the flock in the care of a shepherd, loaded up and set out, as Jesse had directed. He reached the camp as the army was going out to its battle positions, shouting the war cry."
—I Samuel 17:20, NIV

There are hundreds of reasons we can deduce on why David held a special place in the heart of God, and one of the earliest we can see is that he was a leader who cared, whether it was for animals or men. Jesse said to his son David to take food supplies to his brothers who were at the battle field fighting the Philistines and bring back assurance from them. The Bible records that the first thing David did was to leave the flock in the care of a shepherd before setting out. This is mostly because a leader cares about those who are under his control and never leaves them at the mercy of the elements or evil. Along the line, you will discover that one of the first things his oldest brother Eliab would inquire about would be if he left the sheep in the wildness; if so, it shows he was conceited and wicked at heart. In other words, that's the description given to a leader who shows no love to the sheep he leads; he is conceited and wicked, but David was neither, because godly leaders care about all they are entrusted with and defend the same sometimes at the expense of all. The gem here is that caring is second nature for a godly leader; if you don't have care in your DNA, you have no business with leadership. God cares for all of his creation, and as a leader, so must you.

- 💎 99 -

UNAPOLOGETIC FOR THE REWARD

"David asked the men standing near him, "What will be done for the man who kills this Philistine and removes this disgrace from Israel? Who is this uncircumcised Philistine that he should defy the armies of the living God?" They repeated to him what they had been saying and told him, "This is what will be done for the man who kills him."
—I Samuel 17:26, 27, NIV

David was a prototype of a leader, though like every human being, he had his weaknesses, but understanding he had paid the price for preparation unashamedly, he requested the reward due to him. He heard the soldiers speak about the great wealth, marriage to the princess, and an exemption from taxes for his family in Israel. David immediately repeated what the reward would be, and the people repeated the same.

Leaders should never be unapologetic about the reward they deserve; this is not in any way covetous or greedy; it is a set pattern, and you should not hold up any false humility to deny a reward expressly stated and not demanded. The gem here is that godly leaders are at liberty to enjoy the rewards that are publicly declared for whatever achievements by their effort they conjure up, which give those being led an advantage.

- 💎 100 -

LEADERS LOOK FOR OPPORTUNITIES TO MANIFEST

"David said to Saul, "Let no one lose heart on account of this Philistine; your servant will go and fight him." Saul replied, "You are not able to go out against this Philistine and fight him; you are only a young man, and he has been a warrior from his youth." But David said to Saul, "Your servant has been keeping his father's sheep. When a lion or a bear came and carried off a sheep from the flock, I went after it, struck it and rescued the sheep from its mouth. When it turned on me, I seized it by its hair, struck it and killed it. Your servant has killed both the lion and the bear; this uncircumcised Philistine will be like one of them, because he has defied the armies of the living God. The Lord who rescued me from the paw of the lion and the paw of the bear will rescue me from the hand of this Philistine." Saul said to David, "Go, and the Lord be with you."
—I Samuel 17:32-37, NIV

Goliath had just presented the young shepherd boy an opportunity to announce himself. Appearing in the valley of Elah, after taking supplies to his brother, David saw Goliath, the Philistine champion from Gath, stepping out from his lines and shouting his usual defiance at the armies of Israel, leaving them dismayed and terrified. He presented himself to be the one to face off with the enemy, and he sensed an opportunity.

When questioned about his credentials, he was quick to replay events of protecting his father's sheep from a lion and a bear. I doubt if many men on the battle field had such an experience. These events assured David that he could rescue the nation from the giant of Gath. His age did not validate capacity, but his experience was the much-needed impetus needed for him to take up the opportunity to manifest. The gem is leaders are never slack in manifesting; there is a moment that comes and godly leaders must discern the opportunity to rise from the dung hill and ride on horses.

- 💎 101 -

WHAT HAVE YOU PROVEN

"And Saul armed David with his armour, and he put an helmet of brass upon his head; also he armed him with a coat of mail. And David girded his sword upon his armour, and he assayed to go; for he had not proved it. And David said unto Saul, I cannot go with these; for I have not proved them. And David put them off him. And he took his staff in his hand, and chose him five smooth stones out of the brook, and put them in a shepherd's bag which he had, even in a scrip; and his sling was in his hand: and he drew near to the Philistine."
—*I Samuel 17:38-40 KJV*

A leader who tries what he has not proven may fall down in shame and ridicule, and David understood this gem quite well. After King Saul had given in to hand over the survival of his people to the young shepherd boy who had no military experience but some backwater tussle with two wild beasts, he was quick to mention that he had no experience using the battle items.

As a wise leader, he averted a risk by seeking out five smooth pebbles, which he put in his bag and, with his sling, approached the arrogant warrior from Gath. Many leaders attempt strategies that leave them in the mud because they want to utilize methodology that they have not yet proven, and for anything you haven't practiced, you can't display mastery. It is little wonder the result of the encounter though must have been a huge surprise to everyone, except David, who knew, apart from the spiritual backing, he had proven what he was walking into battle with.

The gem here is that godly leaders must be conscious and realistic about what they are good at, their area of expertise, and work on other areas they are not good at. Leaders must prove this in private first before making a public appearance.

- ◈ 102 -

LEADERS UNDERSTAND THE COVENANT IN OPERATION OVER THEIR JURISDICTION

"This day will the LORD deliver thee into mine hand; and I will smite thee, and take thine head from thee; and I will give the carcases of the host of the Philistines this day unto the fowls of the air, and to the wild beasts of the earth; that all the earth may know that there is a God in Israel. And all this assembly shall know that the LORD saveth not with sword and spear: for the battle is the LORD's, and he will give you into our hands."
—*I Samuel 17:46-47 KJV*

You could picture the young David exuding an unusual confidence that could have been interpreted as arrogance by onlookers; he approached Goliath with just pebbles riding on the back of his encounters with wild animals. The future King of Israel was empowered by his understanding of the covenant in operation over Israel. Dating back to Abraham, God instituted the commandment of circumcision, speaking to the patriarch that the covenant was going to be between him and all his male seed; as such, it guaranteed God's intervention in their affairs.

This gave David the impetus to address the giant of Gath as an uncircumcised philistine, thus establishing spiritual authority over him. He would assure him that he would fall and his head taken from him, while a buffet would await the fowls of the air and beasts of the earth with his unguarded remains. Leaders must walk in knowledge to excel; they must not be ignorant of spiritual laws that play over the location and jurisdiction, or even the people they lead. Ignorance of this will make an already tough job even harder. The gem is that godly leaders endeavor to understand the covenant, if any, in operation over their scope and areas of leadership.

- 💎 103 -

FINISHING THE JOB

"Therefore David ran, and stood upon the Philistine, and took his sword, and drew it out of the sheath thereof, and slew him, and cut off his head therewith. And when the Philistines saw their champion was dead, they fled."
—I Samuel 17:51 KJV

David was a finisher by all accounts, living up to the expectations of leaders who know their onus. Goliath of Gath lay on the bare floor of the valley of Elah, probably wondering how the smooth pebbles got buried in his forehead. Lying down, unable to move a limb and blinded by the hot, scorching sun, he heard the celebratory sounds of the Israelites but none from his colleagues. As David stood over him, temporarily blotting out the sun from his view, the last thing Goliath remembered was the reflection of light on a metal blade.

David understood that it is never over until it is; he made sure he finished the job he signed up for. Every time you leave a task almost done, you run the risk of it resurrecting to probably cause far greater harm. The gem is to be like David: cut off the head of all you are called to do and finish the job.

- 💎 104 -

JEALOUSY

"And it came to pass as they came, when David was returned from the slaughter of the Philistine, that the women came out of all cities of Israel, singing and dancing, to meet king Saul, with tabrets, with joy, and with instruments of musick. And the women answered one another as they played, and said, Saul hath slain his thousands, And David his ten thousands. And Saul was very wroth, and the saying displeased him; and he said, They have ascribed unto David ten thousands, and to me they have ascribed but thousands: and what can he have more but the kingdom? And Saul eyed David from that day and forward."
—I Samuel 18:6-9, KJV

Saul was never a green-eyed monster; there was no record that he ever suffered from jealousy prior to the emergence of David on the political scene. It can be tough for many leaders when others start receiving praise they believe should justifiably be theirs. The Israeli army was returning from the battle; a victory parade was well on the way; the people must have hung from windows and balconies singing praises. Then, with musical instruments creating melodious tunes, Saul would immediately pay closer attention to the lyrics of the maidens and young men who lined up the route to the royal palace. Saul hath slain his thousands and David his ten thousands. The Sheer audacity and insult pelted at the king at that moment, caused a deed whose fruit never offers the leader sweetness, but only bitterness was sown in his heart.

Saul was wroth and was displeased, and it is said from that day forward he eyed David and sought to do away with him. Leaders must be very careful when it comes to the sensitive issue of jealousy. We often tell ourselves it can never be us because we possess the emotional and mental strength when we are compared to others or our achievements are put side by side with those of others, but it is a fallacy; it takes an unusual help from God to be rid of any jealous feeling that can creep up at any moment. The gem here is that godly leaders must by all means resist and fight any stirring of jealousy. I have noticed leaders who, like Saul, start exhibiting traits of delusion and other physiological imbalances; sometimes it gets so overwhelming they trust no one, except yes men who agree with their every word. Everyone is a potential enemy seeking to bring them down. With all of these, it is nearly impossible for such a leader to deliver on the goods while looking over their shoulder and obsessively worried about who is perceived to be better than them. You seek to lead in a manner pleasing to God avoid the plague of jealousy.

- 💎 105 -

SUCCESS IN ALL HIS WAYS

> *"In everything he did he had great success, because the Lord was with him. When Saul saw how successful he was, he was afraid of him. But all Israel and Judah loved David, because he led them in their campaigns. The Philistine commanders continued to go out to battle, and as often as they did, David met with more success than the rest of Saul's officers, and his name became well known."*
> — I Samuel 18:14-16, 30, NIV

David possesses a godly character that all leaders found in the Bible exhibited and which will be a recurring decimal through this book, and that is the presence of God that guarantees success. In everything that David undertook to do, it was met with great success because the presence of the Lord was with him. The presence was the difference, and all of the country loved him, primarily because people like following successful leaders with results to show for it.

If you are a leader with no verifiable and tangible track record of success, it is only a matter of time before those you lead become disillusioned and frustrated. David led them in many campaigns, recording a string of victories, and the more the Philistine commanders went out to battle, the more success he recorded. At a point he was high on the victory score card of all of the officers of the Israeli army,

238

and one noticeable attribute of success is the fame that heralds it, but the difference was the Lord was with him; if you make a demand for great success, you cannot travel on that road without a higher authority teleprompting your activities and granting grace. Godly leaders must never walk the pathway without the presence of the Lord; the gem is essential to embrace because you need an all-powerful, all-knowing companion to achieve success in all your ways.

- 💎 106 -

RELATED WELL WITH PEOPLE AROUND HIM

"But Jonathan Saul's son delighted much in David: and Jonathan told David, saying, Saul my father seeketh to kill thee: now therefore, I pray thee, take heed to thyself until the morning, and abide in a secret place, and hide thyself: And Jonathan spake good of David unto Saul his father, and said unto him, Let not the king sin against his servant, against David; because he hath not sinned against thee, and because his works have been to thee-ward very good."
—I Samuel 19:2, 4, KJV

"And David saw that Saul was come out to seek his life: and David was in the wilderness of Ziph in a wood. And Jonathan Saul's son arose, and went to David into the wood, and strengthened his hand in God. And he said unto him, Fear not: for the hand of Saul my father shall not find thee; and thou shalt be king over Israel, and I shall be next unto thee; and that also Saul my father knoweth. And they two made a covenant before the LORD: and David abode in the wood, and Jonathan went to his house."
—I Samuel 23:15-18, KJV

The story of the bromance between David and Jonathan is one for the ages, an heir apparent pushing aside what could have been described as his birth right and giving support and unbridled love to the very individual who would take his place. When brooding over this story, beyond the fact that I sense that Jonathan clearly perceived that God's hand was on David and he was the chosen successor to his father, it is evident that David related well with people, and Jonathan was not an exception. Many leaders have a nasty attitude when it comes to dealing with others. The hand of God may be on you to provide leadership to your generation, but if you have an attitude problem and struggle to relate positively with others, that call will be hampered and frustrated.

Godly leaders must constantly X-ray their relatability index, they must humble themselves to get constructive feedback to improve. Jonathan delighted so much in David to the point of defending him before and shielding him from his father. The gem here is that godly leaders never underestimate how they treat people. David wasn't doing this because Jonathan was a prince but because he was a human being. You shouldn't treat people because of their status but mostly because God expects you to relate well with all people. His relatability is one that built a covenant brotherhood we draw inspiration from to this day.

- 💎 107 -

SEASONS OF PREPARATION

"David therefore departed thence, and escaped to the cave Adullam: and when his brethren and all his father's house heard it, they went down thither to him. And every one that was in distress, and every one that was in debt, and every one that was discontented, gathered themselves unto him; and he became a captain over them: and there were with him about four hundred men."
—*I Samuel 22:1, 2, KJV*

The chosen one had been declared persona non grata in Israel; the King had finally snapped and would have nothing but the head of David on a platter or even better in a basket. David read the mood in the palace; his closest advisers and his best friend would have sent word that the King had asked for him to be murdered, his home was no longer a safe haven, the streets had become a snare, the city had become a cauldron, and he had no option but to flee. David immediately departed and escaped to the now famous crucible of preparation, the cave of Adullam. He was now a fugitive with no help horizontally but only vertical from above. David at the moment never could have seen that the cave was part of the preparation that God intended; when he was there, it is said that his brethren and all his father's house went down to him, but others were attracted to him, those who were in distress, everyone who was in debt, and everyone who was discontented, and in that cave he became a captain over them.

I doubt that those men knew the university they were signing for, they sought succour along with their leader, who was on the wanted list, but this was a season of preparation. David understood that leaders don't waste seasons, and he put it to great use by allowing the men to undergo the much needed leadership training that would support his kingship. Godly leaders must appreciate such seasons like David.

You must, while prayerfully seeking growth and empowerment, improve yourself and those around you. It is the same individuals who were described in the most uncharitable terms that the Bible will re-introduce as the mighty men of David. Every leader will be confronted with a season where, if utilized, can shake off the impurities and impediments to successful leadership. Embrace your often hard seasons; they are often times cloaked by difficulties, when in essence their mission is to ensure there is a birthing of a leader who can handle all seasons; the one who cannot be stressed or stretched cannot be made a chief or a king.

- 💎 108 -

AN ENQUIRING LEADER

"Therefore David enquired of the LORD, saying, Shall I go and smite these Philistines? And the LORD said unto David, Go, and smite the Philistines, and save Keilah. Then David enquired of the LORD yet again. And the LORD answered him and said, Arise, go down to Keilah; for I will deliver the Philistines into thine hand. Then said David, Will the men of Keilah deliver me and my men into the hand of Saul? And the LORD said, They will deliver thee up."
— I Samuel 23:2, 4, 12, KJV

How many times have you made decisions whose results came back to bite you on the backside? I know I have. As a leader, I have rushed into taking actions justifiable and wise in my eyes, but I realized that I jumped right into error. The best of leaders are enquiring ones, those who understand that they must have all the facts, and even in the presence of that, they rely on the Holy Spirit to take certain decisions. David was a leader who enquired, and this saved him from ending on a stake or falling in battle.

His men showed fear, asking how their small band would go against the forces, and once again he enquired of the Lord, who assured him of victory. Even after securing victory and upon hearing that Saul was hot on his heels, believing he had imprisoned himself in the fotress of Keilah, he immediately spoke to Abiathar the priest, asking for the ephod. He made another inquiry about whether Saul would come down and if he was going to be betrayed by the citizens of that city, and the Lord answered in affirmative. For this reason, he fled with six hundred of his men, and when Saul was told he had escaped, he did not go there. The gem here is that successful leaders are those who ask questions. You can imagine if David relied solely on his own intelligence, he surely would have had his life come to an abrupt end by Saul and his forces. Godly leaders constantly make enquiries about situations around them. In your leadership journey, you will come to realize that nothing is too small or too big to bring before God.

- 💎 109 -

LEADERS PATHWAY WAS MUST BE HONOURABLE

"*And he came to the sheepcotes by the way, where was a cave; and Saul went in to cover his feet: and David and his men remained in the sides of the cave. And the men of David said unto him, Behold the day of which the LORD said unto thee, Behold, I will deliver thine enemy into thine hand, that thou mayest do to him as it shall seem good unto thee. Then David arose, and cut off the skirt of Saul's robe privily. And it came to pass afterward, that David's heart smote him, because he had cut off Saul's skirt. And he said unto his men, The LORD forbid that I should do this thing unto my master, the LORD's anointed, to stretch forth mine hand against him, seeing he is the anointed of the LORD. So David stayed his servants with these words, and suffered them not to rise against Saul. But Saul rose up out of the cave, and went on his way. David also arose afterward, and went out of the cave, and cried after Saul, saying, My Lord the king. And when Saul looked behind him, David stooped with his face to the earth, and bowed himself. And David said to Saul, Wherefore hearest thou men's words, saying, Behold, David seeketh thy hurt? Behold, this day thine eyes have seen how that the LORD had delivered thee to day into mine hand in the cave: and some bade me kill thee: but mine eye spared thee; and I said, I will not put forth mine hand against my Lord; for he is the LORD's anointed. Moreover, my father, see, yea, see the skirt of thy robe in my hand: for in that I cut off the skirt of thy robe, and killed thee not, know thou*

and see that there is neither evil nor transgression in mine hand, and I have not sinned against thee; yet thou huntest my soul to take it. And he said to David, Thou art more righteous than I: for thou hast rewarded me good, whereas I have rewarded thee evil. And thou hast shewed this day how that thou hast dealt well with me: forasmuch as when the LORD had delivered me into thine hand, thou killedst me not. For if a man find his enemy, will he let him go well away? wherefore the LORD reward thee good for that thou hast done unto me this day. And now, behold, I know well that thou shalt surely be king, and that the kingdom of Israel shall be established in thine hand. Swear now therefore unto me by the LORD, that thou wilt not cut off my seed after me, and that thou wilt not destroy my name out of my father's house. And David sware unto Saul. And Saul went home; but David and his men gat them up unto the hold."
—I Samuel 24:3-11, 17-22, KJV

There is a common saying in the world that "the end justifies the means." As a result, leaders often resort to using any means necessary to reach the top. This often results in leaders selling their souls in order to secure their position of power. Godly leaders must understand that their pathway to leading must be honourable; this itself possesses an inherent sustaining power for the leader void of guilt, negativity, etc. Saul was close to finally catching his arch-enemy, that annoying young shepherd whose fame had been on the rise from the day; he was lucky enough to have his pebble stones slay the Giant of Gath and his equally successful expeditions, winning battles against those pesky Philistine soldiers whose military training must have diminished with the way they lose to David. He would no longer take the disgrace, and by any means possible, David must be captured and disgraced, and Saul must be present to witness it firsthand.

In one instance, Saul was hibernating in a cave, oblivious that David and his men were in the same cave. The men following David were elated, finally, the hunter was about to be captured by the prey, but David elected to instead cut a piece of Saul's robe while he was asleep. Speaking to his men, he mentioned that touching the Lord's anointed was a display of dishonor. Afterwards, he moved to a safe distance and summoned Saul. He reenacted a scenario in which he could have immediately put an end to the assault and persecution he was facing, but he refused to use a nefarious act as a means to ascend to the throne.

The gem here is that godly leaders must be very intentional that their rise to leadership position must be done in a godly manner. Allow God to place you there, not by scheming, manipulating, or eliminating competition; the way you ascend will reveal much about your leadership style. Set a tone that will allow your leadership to lead with integrity.

- 💎 110 -

NO COWARDICE IN RETREAT

"But David thought to himself, "One of these days I will be destroyed by the hand of Saul. The best thing I can do is to escape to the land of the Philistines. Then Saul will give up searching for me anywhere in Israel, and I will slip out of his hand." So David and the six hundred men with him left and went over to Achish son of Maok king of Gath."
—I Samuel 27:1, 2, NIV

Leaders must understand that despite what a lot of people believe there is nothing wrong with a retreat, it may be interpreted by many as cowardice by anyone relaying the story, but it is said that a living dog is better than a dead lion. David found himself in a challenging situation; Saul was relentless in his pursuit of the son of Jesse, and the constant pursuit can be quite draining. Remember David was anointed by the great Prophet Samuel for the throne? Was it all a dream? Despite the call for leadership, he said to himself in wisdom, one of these days I will be destroyed by the hand of Saul, and he decided that the best place he could run was the very country where he was a wanted man.

David would rather be in the hands of the eternal enemies of Isreal than to face his own king and countryman, and besides, he knew that Saul would not give up chasing him, so he and his wandering men went to Achish, king of Gath (the hometown of their most favourite son Goliath). Godly leaders, it's crucial to understand that there is wisdom in retreating. Don't succumb to the misconception that leaders should mentally envision themselves as Napoleon or Alexander the Great, leading men into battle, rather than retreating into seclusion. There is no cowardice in retreat when you could suffer an inevitable defeat.

- 💎 111 -

WITTY TO SURVIVE

"When Achish asked, "Where did you go raiding today?" David would say, "Against the Negev of Judah" or "Against the Negev of Jerahmeel" or "Against the Negev of the Kenites." He did not leave a man or woman alive to be brought to Gath, for he thought, "They might inform on us and say, 'This is what David did.'" And such was his practice as long as he lived in Philistine territory. Achish trusted David and said to himself, "He has become so obnoxious to his people, the Israelites, that he will be my servant for life."
— *I Samuel 27:10-12, NIV*

Sometimes leaders need to employ witty strategies to stay alive, and there is absolutely nothing wrong with this. David was now living in exile with the Philistines, the sworn enemies of his birth country, because King Saul had sworn to murder the young man. He was given the town of Ziklag, which had belonged to the Kings of Judah ever since. To prove his loyalty to Achish, he realized that he needed to do things that were needed to ensure that he never lost the head on his shoulders either to Saul or to Achish. Every time he was asked where he had gone raiding, he would say against the Negev of Judah or of Jerahmeel or Kenites to win over Achish, when in reality he and his men went up and raided the Geshurites, the Girzites, and the Amalekites, and whenever he struck, he ensured he left no human alive and took all their animals and belongings.

For this reason, Achish trusted David, believing that he had become extremely unpleasant to his own people and would remain a servant to him. Though mischievous, one must consider the rather unpleasant scenario that destiny had plunged him into, and for this reason survival was imperative. As a godly leader, there may be scenarios where you may find yourself by the hand that life has dealt you. The gem here is that you may need to employ some witty strategies to avoid being consumed. Sometimes this may be the only option available to you as a leader; therefore, you must, like David, also have the ability to think on your feet and also pull out a joker from your pack of cards.

- 💎 112 -

TIMES OF DISTRESS

"David and his men reached Ziklag on the third day. Now the Amalekites had raided the Negev and Ziklag. They had attacked Ziklag and burned it, and had taken captive the women and everyone else in it, both young and old. They killed none of them, but carried them off as they went on their way. David was greatly distressed because the men were talking of stoning him; each one was bitter in spirit because of his sons and daughters. But David found strength in the Lord his God. Then David said to Abiathar the priest, the son of Ahimelek, "Bring me the ephod." Abiathar brought it to him, and David inquired of the Lord, "Shall I pursue this raiding party? Will I overtake them?" "Pursue them," he answered. "You will certainly overtake them and succeed in the rescue."
—*I Samuel 30:1-2, 6-8, NIV*

Every leader must know that there will be days where it seems the entire world has conspired together to visit distress on you, days when questions will be asked and you may never be given the privilege of an answer. David had a day (one of so many) when his world almost came crashing down. He and his men had ridden out with the Philistines to fight the Israelites. During the review of the men by the Lords of the Philistines, a question was asked on why Hebrew men were in their ranks, despite Achish swearing to the loyalty of David (who I am sure at this point was helpless on what was to happen, and God was stirring something to avoid David slaying his own countrymen who he was to later rule).

The men clearly distrusted David, pretty positive that he may attempt to regain the trust of Saul by turning on them in the heat of battle. After reassuring words from Achish, David and his men embarked on a three-day journey to return to Ziklag. Upon arriving, they discovered their camp had been raided by the Amalekites and completely burnt down, and all the people were taken captive, with none killed. David, like a true leader, was completely distraught and must have been a mental wreck, and his men started speaking about stoning him, and quite instructively, he found strength in the Lord God.

Like we analyzed earlier on the inquisitiveness of godly leaders, David called for the ephod and got the heavenly flag of to pursue, overtake, and recover, which was what happened. Though the gleaming gem here is that leaders must prepare for times of distress, when even your own people may seek to stone you, never take this to heart, always reminding yourself that the best of men is nothing but a man.

One of my favourite authors, Bob Sorge, speaks about servant leaders drinking deeply of what he calls the lacerating sting of rejection, which will tenderize such an individual to the reality of rejection and help sensitize him to show how easily rejection can be inflicted on others to better handle others with care and tenderness. Distress is a vital ingredient in the training of leaders, and after the training, it continues to be a tool to maintain and guard hearts to remain tender.

- 💎 113 -

TREATING YOUR PEOPLE RIGHT

"They found an Egyptian in a field and brought him to David. They gave him water to drink and food to eat— part of a cake of pressed figs and two cakes of raisins. He ate and was revived, for he had not eaten any food or drunk any water for three days and three nights. David asked him, "Who do you belong to? Where do you come from?" He said, "I am an Egyptian, the slave of an Amalekite. My master abandoned me when I became ill three days ago. We raided the Negev of the Kerethites, some territory belonging to Judah and the Negev of Caleb. And we burned Ziklag." David asked him, "Can you lead me down to this raiding party?" He answered, "Swear to me before God that you will not kill me or hand me over to my master, and I will take you down to them."
—*I Samuel 30:11-15, NIV*

Leaders who do not know how to treat others well will struggle in various ways; the absence of human kindness will always guarantee closed doors. David had been given the green light to chase the Amalekites; remember, they took everyone captive, including his wives and children. On their way, they may have used various tracking methods that warriors and hunters used to track wild animals and human beings. They would stumble on an Egyptian, and rather than being harsh and wicked, they gave him water to drink and food to eat. Immediately he was revived, he gave a first-hand account of what transpired in the raid of Ziklag and how his master abandoned him on the way.

This act will be the open door for the kindness of David to use and walk right in to recover. The Egyptian, after securing his life gave his loyalty and offered to lead the men to the raiding army. Many leaders have faced betrayal due to the way they mistreat people, while other leaders have been able to anchor men down with the heavy weight of kindness (that is not to say, individuals cannot betray despite tasting kindness). The gem here is that godly leaders understand that kindness must be given and used in large quantities even when there is no assurance of a return or exchange for it; it is a seed that will birth a tree and eventually a forest. Don't underestimate treating people right, especially those who serve you.

- 💎 114 -

COMPENSATION

> *"David replied, "No, my brothers, you must not do that with what the Lord has given us. He has protected us and delivered into our hands the raiding party that came against us. Who will listen to what you say? The share of the man who stayed with the supplies is to be the same as that of him who went down to the battle. All will share alike." David made this a statute and ordinance for Israel from that day to this. When David reached Ziklag, he sent some of the plunder to the elders of Judah, who were his friends, saying, "Here is a gift for you from the plunder of the Lord's enemies." David sent it to those who were in Bethel, Ramoth Negev and Jattir; to those in Aroer, Siphmoth, Eshtemoa and Rakal; to those in the towns of the Jerahmeelites and the Kenites; and Hebron; and to those in all the other places where he and his men had roamed."*
> —I Samuel 30:23-29, 31, NIV

David celebrated all and even better compensated his men. With his four hundred men (two hundred had elected to stay back, unable to continue), victory was confirmed, and nothing was missing and everyone recovered. Also, the plunder was far too great. Now upon their return, there was a fight among the men; the victorious men who had fought the battle argued that the great spoil wasn't going to be shared with the two hundred who stayed back.

A justifiable reason by their account, but their leader David showed wisdom in ensuring everyone under his command got compensated. He said to them that the share of the one who stayed with the supplies must be the same as the one who went out to battle, and he made it in ordinance; he did not stop there, he took it further by sending a portion to various towns, cities, and places where he and his men roamed. What a leader! Godly leaders must never be seen to be greedy; otherwise, they will lose their men faster than a Formula One racer. Those being led always have an eye out for generosity and adequate compensation. The gem here as a leader is ensuring everyone under your command is compensated.

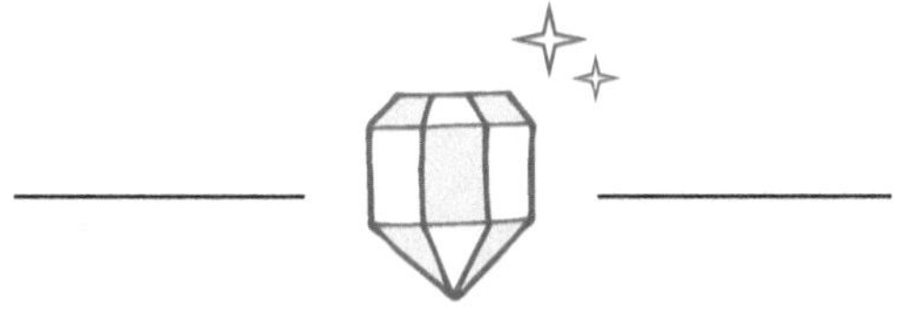

THE BOOK OF
II SAMUEL

- 🛡 115 -

RECONCILIATION

"And the men of Judah came, and there they anointed David king over the house of Judah. And they told David, saying, That the men of Jabesh-gilead were they that buried Saul. And David sent messengers unto the men of Jabesh-gilead, and said unto them, Blessed be ye of the LORD, that ye have shewed this kindness unto your Lord, even unto Saul, and have buried him. And now the LORD shew kindness and truth unto you: and I also will requite you this kindness, because ye have done this thing. Therefore now let your hands be strengthened, and be ye valiant: for your master Saul is dead, and also the house of Judah have anointed me king over them."
—II Samuel 2:4-7, KJV

The book, A Long Walk to Freedom, by South African legend Nelson Mandela springs to mind here, after serving about twenty-seven years in prison, by divine providence he would become president, and instead of visiting vengeance on those who made him suffer untold physical, mental, emotional, and financial anguish, he instead sought forgiveness and reconciliation. King Saul was dead just like the Prophet Samuel had spoken, along with his sons, and the throne was now finally empty for the anointed David to take over the reins of power. We must remember the House of Saul had sworn allegiance to the dead king and would have, by every stretch of our imagination, visited untold hardship on David.

After the tribe of Judah made David king, the men of Jabesh Gilead had their brave soldiers retrieve Saul's remains from the Philistine temple, where he had been placed as an object of ridicule and buried him. David will reveal to us the powerful gem of reconciliation when you have been hurt by reaching out via emissaries to the House of Saul, blessing them for showing kindness and promising them favour because of the act, and then informing them he had been anointed, even though the immediate olive branch was not fully accepted as there would be war between both the Houses of David and Saul.

We can clearly see how godly leaders should act, and one of the very first action points is reconciliation. Not everyone wants you there; whenever someone rises, there will be others who also covet the same position. It is therefore imperative for a leader to embark on reconciliation to some degree and give a smooth leadership journey

- 🛡 116 -

SEEDS OF DOUBT ON
LOYALTY AND ACCUSATION

"Now Saul had had a concubine named Rizpah daughter of Aiah. And Ish-Bosheth said to Abner, "Why did you sleep with my father's concubine?" Abner was very angry because of what Ish-Bosheth said. So he answered, "Am I a dog's head—on Judah's side? This very day I am loyal to the house of your father Saul and to his family and friends. I haven't handed you over to David. Yet now you accuse me of an offense involving this woman! May God deal with Abner, be it ever so severely, if I do not do for David what the Lord promised him on oath and transfer the kingdom from the house of Saul and establish David's throne over Israel and Judah from Dan to Beersheba." Ish-Bosheth did not dare to say another word to Abner, because he was afraid of him."
—II Samuel 3:7-11, NIV

Leaders must secure and protect loyal individuals, as they are becoming increasingly rare. Abner Son of Ner was the commander of Saul's army, a general who had by all standards proven himself to be a warrior and leader. After the death of his king, he pitched his tent with Ish-Bosheth, the son of Saul, brought him over to Mahanaim, and made him king over Gilead, Ashuri, Jezereel, Ephraim, Benjamin, and all of Israel, leaving only Judah to David. The lucky prince had a man who could have attempted to take the throne for himself, with thousands of soldiers at his beck and call, but instead passed on power, fighting David and his men.

Ish-Bosheth, a young and inexperienced leader, will make a rookie mistake by isolating the one man he needs to secure his kingship. Saul had a concubine named Rizpah, and for whatever reason, he accused his general of sleeping with her. In a sharp response and in anger, Abner rebuked the king, reminding him that he hadn't handed him over to David out of loyalty, but the king had the effrontery to accuse a battle-hardened soldier over a concubine. Instantly he informed the king by swearing hand over the kingdom to David, whom God had promised to establish as king over Israel and Judah.

Leaders must apply wisdom when dealing with loyalists, there are occasions that lines could be crossed and which action must be taken; such action must be systematic and strategic so as not to affect your leadership standing. The gem here is to avoid sowing seeds of doubt on loyalists and be wise in your accusations. A leader is only a leader when he has people who follow him.

- 🛡 117 -

TURNING ENEMIES TO ALLIES

"Then Abner sent messengers on his behalf to say to David, "Whose land is it? Make an agreement with me, and I will help you bring all Israel over to you." "Good," said David. "I will make an agreement with you. But I demand one thing of you: Do not come into my presence unless you bring Michal daughter of Saul when you come to see me." Abner conferred with the elders of Israel and said, "For some time you have wanted to make David your king. Abner also spoke to the Benjamites in person. Then he went to Hebron to tell David everything that Israel and the whole tribe of Benjamin wanted to do. Then David said to Joab and all the people with him, "Tear your clothes and put on sackcloth and walk in mourning in front of Abner." King David himself walked behind the bier. They buried Abner in Hebron, and the king wept aloud at Abner's tomb. All the people wept also."
—II Samuel 3:12, 13, 17, 19, 31-32, NIV

David by this time was already fast becoming politically savvy, and when Abner's message reached him, he responded promptly. Good that he would make an agreement; he was quick to make demands like the return of his wife, but more importantly, a wise leader understands that he must never pass on a golden opportunity to turn enemies into allies. This is not a time to revisit the past and remember past hostilities; the less opposition a leader faces, the greater the likelihood for him to deliver on his mandate of service. Often some leaders may adopt this half-heartedly, and it can be a time bomb likely to go off in the future. David genuinely wanted to have a united kingdom, and his acceptance of the offer was not politically driven alone but was from the pure heart of a leader, which should hold no guile.

This is the fundamental reason he showed genuine pain when Abner was unjustifiably slain in an act of revenge by Joab to avenge the blood of his brother Asahel; the national mourning declared was genuine and intentional, and David joined as the chief mourner. The gem here is that godly leaders must understand that we should constantly be on the lookout for opportunities that present themselves for enemies to turn to allies, just like the wise King David showed.

- 118 -

SINCERITY

"Then they all came and urged David to eat something while it was still day; but David took an oath, saying, "May God deal with me, be it ever so severely, if I taste bread or anything else before the sun sets!" All the people took note and were pleased; indeed, everything the king did pleased them. So on that day all the people there and all Israel knew that the king had no part in the murder of Abner son of Ner."
—II Samuel 3:35-37, NIV

Sincerity is a quality you must present to those you lead. I can only imagine the tabloids in Israel reporting the news that David had conspired with his general, Joab, to finally extinguish his long-time foe and right hand of his predecessor. The editors would have described how David reasoned and how hard it would be for him to rule with the influence that Abner commanded amongst the troops and political elite. Abner had just finished his visit to the King to finalize the terms of power settlement and transfer of authority.

After Abner's departure, Joab arrived, learning that his blood brother's murderer was present and had left unharmed. He entered the king's presence, furious at Abner's escape, accusing him of using deceitful attempt to conquer David.

He won no sympathy from the king, and he proceeded to hatch a plan by having his messengers lure Abner to return to David, livid on how Abner could have escaped with all the strands of hair on him . Without the King's authority, upon his arrival, he took him aside and murdered him.

David, upon hearing this, swore to the heavens that he and his house were innocent over the shedding of blood, declaring that judgement fall on Joab and his family, even issuing a curse that there must always be someone in his family suffering from soreness or leprosy. Apart from partaking in the burial, the musician in him came out singing a lament for the fallen general. To prove his sincerity, he went on a hunger strike, declaring not to eat before the sun set. At this point it was recorded that the people took note. We can see that those we lead take notes on sincerity and insincerity, and they act it out accordingly. The people were pleased with all he did and showed, and they concluded that the King had no part in the murder of Abner. I can imagine the headline the following day by the Israel Chronicles Newspaper: "King David—Innocent of Murder." The gem here is that godly leaders must be sincere in all their dealings, there must be the absence of pretence, deceit, and hypocrisy.

- ◊ 119 -

CAUTION OVER YOUR LIEUTENANTS

*"Then the king said to his men, "Do you not realize
that a commander and a great man has fallen in Israel
this day? And today, though I am the anointed king,
I am weak, and these sons of Zeruiah are too strong
for me. May the Lord repay the evildoer according to
his evil deeds!"*
—II Samuel 3:38, 39, NIV

Many times a leader may find himself surrounded by
ambitious lieutenants that may be difficult to rein in due
to their sacrifice in the leader's ascension, their skill, and
proficiency, etc., and the sons of Zeruiah, Abishai, Joab,
and Asahel, nephews of the King, fall into that category.
In fact, David would declare that they were too strong for
him—not the kind of statement any leader should utter.
While this scenario was more delicate due to blood ties,
you must always be in control of your lieutants, and the
major reason is that their actions will often be interpreted
as having been endorsed and approved by you, and the
buck lies at the feet of the leader at the end of the day.

Leaders who ignore the actions of their lieutenants will rule
over a reign of terror and recklessness. David, understanding
this important fact, would address his men with sincerity,
reaffirming the greatness of the fallen Abner and giving
judgement to God. The gem here is that godly leaders must

first be conscious of those who hold authority figures in their leadership team and ensure that they have only those they can control; they must never be helpless to the point of resigning to faith; the people you lead are watching and seeing your fairness and justice in all manners; be wary of this trap; also constantly caution your lieutants, with the reminder that their actions have the power to reduce your leadership to a pile of rubble. Be wise

- 🛡 120 -

HONOUR TO RIVALS
EVEN TILL DEATH

"They had gone into the house while he was lying on the bed in his bedroom. After they stabbed and killed him, they cut off his head. Taking it with them, they traveled all night by way of the Arabah. They brought the head of Ish-Bosheth to David at Hebron and said to the king, "Here is the head of Ish-Bosheth son of Saul, your enemy, who tried to kill you. This day the Lord has avenged my Lord the king against Saul and his offspring." David answered Rekab and his brother Baanah, the sons of Rimmon the Beerothite, "As surely as the Lord lives, who has delivered me out of every trouble, when someone told me, 'Saul is dead,' and thought he was bringing good news, I seized him and put him to death in Ziklag. That was the reward I gave him for his news! How much more—when wicked men have killed an innocent man in his own house and on his own bed—should I not now demand his blood from your hand and rid the earth of you!" So David gave an order to his men, and they killed them. They cut off their hands and feet and hung the bodies by the pool in Hebron. But they took the head of Ish-Bosheth and buried it in Abner's tomb at Hebron."
—II Samuel 4:7-12, NIV

A matured stance of leaders is honouring their rivals even till death. Today's representation of leaders are those who possess a do-or-die attitude; they are filled with so much hatred for those who oppose them, when God expects us to be beacons of love in such a manner that our leading inspires others to be more like God. With Abner dead, Ish-Bosheth knew he had no chance and had lost all courage; this was clearly sniffed by those around him. Two men who acted as raiders on behalf of Saul, Baanah, and Rekab sensed the wind of change in leadership and, probably to secure their lot, set out for the home of the son of the former king, and upon arrival they went into the bedroom and killed him during his sleep, cutting off his head, and travelled all night to present the remains as a sign of allegiance to David.

Unfortunately, they were meeting a different kind of leader who had no regard for such wicked acts that, though they may appear beneficial to him, dishonour his rivals. He reminded the men of the actions taken against the one who carried just the news of the death of Saul—how much more the ones who killed an innocent man on his bed? Immediately he ordered they be gruesomely put to death and buried the head of Ish-Bosheth. Godly leaders know their leadership is more honourable when perfumed with honour; the gem here is that it pays to honour to all men and is even more dignifying when it is extended to your rivals or perceived enemies. Lead with love.

- 🛡 121 -

STRATEGY BEFORE EFFORT

"The king and his men marched to Jerusalem to attack the Jebusites, who lived there. The Jebusites said to David, "You will not get in here; even the blind and the lame can ward you off." They thought, "David cannot get in here." Nevertheless, David captured the fortress of Zion—which is the City of David. On that day David had said, "Anyone who conquers the Jebusites will have to use the water shaft to reach those 'lame and blind' who are David's enemies." That is why they say, "The 'blind and lame' will not enter the palace." so David inquired of the Lord, "Shall I go and attack the Philistines? Will you deliver them into my hands?" The Lord answered him, "Go, for I will surely deliver the Philistines into your hands." so David inquired of the Lord, and he answered, "Do not go straight up, but circle around behind them and attack them in front of the poplar trees. As soon as you hear the sound of marching in the tops of the poplar trees, move quickly, because that will mean the Lord has gone out in front of you to strike the Philistine army." So David did as the Lord commanded him, and he struck down the Philistines all the way from Gibeon to Gezer."
—II Samuel 5:6-8, 19, 23-25, NIV

A leader is more often than not a strategist by nature, and David buttressed this assertion. The king had his sights set on a new capital. One that would serve as a place where God would also meet his people. He marched to Jerusalem to attack the indigenes, the fiercely independent Canaanite tribe of the Jebusites who were living there, and due to the impregnable topography of the city, the terrain was every invading army's nightmare. The people even taunted David that he would never get in, and even their blind and lame would defend the city, mostly driven by the confidence that nothing could come in or go out.

Leaders are built to crack hard problems and overcome obstacles. In consideration of what must have been times spent in prayer plus the reports from reconnaissance, he offered a reward to anyone willing to undertake what was clearly a suicide attempt. Some men would take the defenders by surprise by climbing up a narrow vertical shaft and sloping tunnel that allowed the people to haul water from the Gihon Spring into their city on top of Ophelia Hill. After the capture, he remained in the city of David, and the ridge on which it stood was renamed Mount Zion.

Another example would also show why a strategist leader is worthy of the crown he wears. The pesky Philistines had come and spread out in the valley of Rephaim, and God showed how strategy always comes before effort. Upon enquiring, God told him not to attack the enemies straight up but rather circle around behind them and attack them in front of the Poplar trees, and he secured a major victory. The gem here is that godly leaders understand that strategy must precede effort. The reason many leaders are making major mistakes and committing blunder is that we put effort before strategy, the cart before the horse. Be wise, seek knowledge on strategy, and the effort will just be a fulfillment.

- 💎 122 -

GOD FIRST

"After the king was settled in his palace and the Lord had given him rest from all his enemies around him, he said to Nathan the prophet, "Here I am, living in a house of cedar, while the ark of God remains in a tent." But that night the word of the Lord came to Nathan, saying: "Go and tell my servant David, 'This is what the Lord says: Are you the one to build me a house to dwell in? I have not dwelt in a house from the day I brought the Israelites up out of Egypt to this day. I have been moving from place to place with a tent as my dwelling. Wherever I have moved with all the Israelites, did I ever say to any of their rulers whom I commanded to shepherd my people Israel, "Why have you not built me a house of cedar?" Now then, tell my servant David, 'This is what the Lord Almighty says: I took you from the pasture, from tending the flock, and appointed you ruler over my people Israel. I have been with you wherever you have gone, and I have cut off all your enemies from before you. Now I will make your name great, like the names of the greatest men on earth. And I will provide a place for my people Israel and will plant them so that they can have a home of their own and no longer be disturbed. Wicked people will not oppress them anymore, as they did at the beginning and have done ever since the time I appointed leaders over my people Israel. I will also give you rest from all your enemies. The Lord declares to you that the Lord himself will establish a house for you: When your days are over and you rest with your ancestors, I will raise up your

offspring to succeed you, your own flesh and blood, and I will establish his kingdom. He is the one who will build a house for my Name, and I will establish the throne of his kingdom forever. I will be his father, and he will be my son. When he does wrong, I will punish him with a rod wielded by men, with floggings inflicted by human hands. But my love will never be taken away from him, as I took it away from Saul, whom I removed from before you. Your house and your kingdom will endure forever before me; your throne will be established forever.' "
—II Samuel 7:1, 2, 4-16, NIV

There is something unique about leaders who understand God must come first; such individuals reap immeasurable and unquantifiable rewards. King David had done it all; he had come a long way from the harsh jungle looking over sheep and becoming a champion of Israel, becoming an outcast, and finally now king over all of Israel. He had been given the ultimate gift every leader craves: rest from all enemies round about him. In this season of reflection, where mostly leaders will spend the time to engage in activities of self-reward, David still put God first. Speaking to Nathan the prophet, he expressed his displeasure with how he was living in a house of cedar and the ark of God remained in a tent. The reply from God was powerful. God opened the volumes of the book reminding David of his origin and the sojourn of the Israelites after leaving Egypt, then he gave what his response is to a leader who puts him first; he promised him greatness, and then he gave the people hope that he will reside in a house built by hands but not that of the king because of his blood-stained hands and entered an eternal covenant of remembrance with the house of David. I have studied leaders, and it is instructive to stress that those who overcame were the ones who put God first in all their dealings. The gem here is that leaders, regardless of the season they find themselves in, find it essential that God must first precede everything. It is tempting to seek personal comfort, and though there is nothing wrong with that, in the heart of a leader must be the consciousness that God must always come first.

- 🛡 123 -

CELEBRATION

"As the ark of the Lord was entering the City of David, Michal daughter of Saul watched from a window. And when she saw King David leaping and dancing before the Lord, she despised him in her heart. When David returned home to bless his household, Michal daughter of Saul came out to meet him and said, "How the king of Israel has distinguished himself today, going around half-naked in full view of the slave girls of his servants as any vulgar fellow would!" David said to Michal, "It was before the Lord, who chose me rather than your father or anyone from his house when he appointed me ruler over the Lord's people Israel—I will celebrate before the Lord."
— II Samuel 6:16, 20, 21, NIV

Leaders have a spirit of celebration that is so infectious, they use joy to draw from the well of salvation; such individuals hardly have a root of bitterness in them because it is the most potent robber of destiny. The Ark of God had been away for a while after the unfortunate incident carrying it from the house of Abinadab. While the celebration was ongoing with the variety of musical instruments raising praise, the oxen stumbled, and Uzzah tried to stabilize it. Unfortunately, because of the irreverent act, he was struck dead, and the procession was suspended. The ark was kept in the household of Obed-Edom for three months.

After David was informed, plans were made for its grand entry into the city of David, this time with all the caution and reverence to escort it. But the most important part of the event lined up was a leader's celebration. It is said David danced so much that his wife Michal watched him from her window and despised him because of his celebration, accusing him that he was acting in an undignified manner before slave girls. David, in wisdom, understood that celebration before God carries in it a spiritual sustenance that upholds leaders and reminded his foolish wife that the choice of a leader is a prerogative of God himself, remembering how he picked him over her father Saul, and for that reason he would keep celebrating before the Lord.

Wise and godly leaders must adopt this celebration posture David had; you must understand that it is an election of his mercy and love that he bestowed on you a responsibility to lead others. The gem here is that leaders must never stop giving praise to the one who placed authority on them; forgetting this important fact is the fastest way to lose the same. Remember, even the twenty and four elders around the throne of God, in reverence for the Lord, cast their crowns down. Leaders, before men, your crown can be on the ground; before God, it must always be cast on the ground.

- ◌ 124 -

JUSTICE AND RIGHTEOUSNESS

"David reigned over all Israel, doing what was just and right for all his people. Joab son of Zeruiah was over the army; Jehoshaphat son of Ahilud was recorder; Zadok son of Ahitub and Ahimelek son of Abiathar were priests; Seraiah was secretary; Benaiah son of Jehoiada was over the Kerethites and Pelethites; and David's sons were priests."
—II Samuel 8:15-18, NIV

The first time I received this gem of advice was when I accepted leadership of a community. Upon visiting one of the homes, an elderly gentleman reminded me to lead according to God's standard, upholding the pillars of justice and righteousness – in other words, to be just and right.

This means treating people in an equitable and fair manner, and being upright. David, who reigned over all of Israel, ruling over countless people, exercised his leadership by doing what was just and right, not just for his tribe, loyalists, or the Adullam crew, but for all his people.

David ensured his leadership benefited everyone, and we must adopt this approach to be effective leaders. Notice how he enforced his leadership style with competent men manning strategic units, keeping the wheels turning.

The gem here is: a leader who is not just and right will suffer grave consequences in their leadership.

- 🛡 125 -

REMEMBRANCE OF KINDNESS

"David asked, "Is there anyone still left of the house of Saul to whom I can show kindness for Jonathan's sake?" "Don't be afraid," David said to him, "for I will surely show you kindness for the sake of your father Jonathan. I will restore to you all the land that belonged to your grandfather Saul, and you will always eat at my table."
—II Samuel 9:1, 7, NIV

"In the course of time, the king of the Ammonites died, and his son Hanun succeeded him as king. David thought, "I will show kindness to Hanun son of Nahash, just as his father showed kindness to me." So David sent a delegation to express his sympathy to Hanun concerning his father. When David's men came to the land of the Ammonites..."
—II Samuel 10:1-2, NIV

David's approach, characterized by justice and righteousness, also gave rise to a kind heart. Following Saul's and Jonathan's deaths, David exhibited a spirit of remembrance of kindness, a unique quality of God, who rewards kindness by opening the book of remembrance.

David asked his courtiers and officials if anyone from the House of Saul was alive, so he could show kindness for Jonathan's sake. Mephibosheth was found, and David restored his grandfather Saul's land and invited him to dine at the king's table.

This act wasn't an emotional one-off. After Nahash, the Ammonite King, passed away, his son Hanun succeeded him. David sent a delegation to express sympathy, intending to show kindness due to Nahash's past actions.

The gem here is: Godly leaders always open their book of remembrance and show kindness to those who paid a huge price or sacrificed without expectation of reward during their ascension journey. This Godly character trait and fruit demonstrates we are indeed like our Father in heaven.

- 126 -

WARY OF THE SPRING SEASON

"One evening David got up from his bed and walked around on the roof of the palace. From the roof he saw a woman bathing. The woman was very beautiful, and David sent someone to find out about her. The man said, "She is Bathsheba, the daughter of Eliam and the wife of Uriah the Hittite." Then David sent messengers to get her. She came to him, and he slept with her. (Now she was purifying herself from her monthly uncleanness.) Then she went back home."
—II Samuel 11:2, 4, NIV

I liken the spring season to one of indulgence, where leaders, unaware, may fall prey to temptations due to its relaxed nature. Though this is when Kings go off to war and not be idle, David had sent General Joab out with the King's men and the whole Israelite army to destroy the Ammonites and to besiege Rabbah, but he remained in Jerusalem.

One faithful day, he would fall victim of a snare that will dent his otherwise immaculate credentials of leadership. He got up from bed and, walking around the roof of the palace, saw a woman bathing. She was beautiful, and soon he would enquire of her, and he sent for her, leading to sexual relations, and afterwards sending her home.

This singular springtime action would cascade into generational consequences that will include bloodshed and death.

The gem here is that leaders must be wary of relaxed seasons of life, when their defenses are down. I want to assume that the presence of the King's men may have made the unholy alliance a lot more difficult to execute. You must ensure you have individuals always around who are not yes-men, but can sound off the warning bells when temptation seeks to lure you away.

Godly leaders, do not, when you should be out at war, be lazing around the roof of the palace. Create guardrails around you, but most importantly, be wary of relaxed moments in life.

- 🛡 127 -

COVETOUSNESS

"When Uriah's wife heard that her husband was dead, she mourned for him. After the time of mourning was over, David had her brought to his house, and she became his wife and bore him a son. But the thing David had done displeased the Lord."
—II Samuel 11:26, 27, NIV

Covetousness is defined as a strong wish to have something, especially something that belongs to someone else, driven by greed and an insatiable desire. Unfortunately, leaders exhibit this dangerous trait, bringing about negative consequences that outweigh the momentary moments of delight when they get what covetousness attracts.

David had sighted Bathsheba, the daughter of Eliam and wife of Uriah the Hittite, naked, and coveted her. After sleeping with her, he received word that she was pregnant. Realizing he was in serious trouble, he sent word to Joab to send Uriah home, under the guise of getting information on the welfare of the army. He would then request him to go home, with the hope that he would have relations with his wife, but instead, he slept at the palace entrance instead of his bed, knowing his colleagues were out on the battlefield.

On the second day, he made him eat and drink, and still, he remained among the servants. David would then hatch the most wicked plan of his kingship by writing to Joab to place Uriah where the fighting was the fiercest and for the army to withdraw to guarantee a certain death.

He would receive a word from Joab about the success of his plan, and when Bathsheba heard the news, she would observe the statutory mourning, and then David brought her into his house, and she became his wife. But what David had done displeased the Lord.

Many biblical leaders fell at the hurdle of covetousness; many of his descendants would commit the same sin. Modern Godly leaders must understand that time has not eclipsed the existence of this spirit; it is very much alive and well. The allure of things, whether human or material, can sway a leader to commit crimes against God and man, totally discrediting them.

The gem here is that you must be wary and cultivate contentment. Contentment is the great antidote towards covetousness. Once a leader lives within the realm of contentment, the claws of covetousness will have no area to grip the soul of a leader.

- 128 -

REPENTANCE

"He must pay for that lamb four times over, because he did such a thing and had no pity." Then Nathan said to David, "You are the man! This is what the Lord, the God of Israel, says: 'I anointed you king over Israel, and I delivered you from the hand of Saul. I gave your master's house to you, and your master's wives into your arms. I gave you all Israel and Judah. And if all this had been too little, I would have given you even more. Why did you despise the word of the Lord by doing what is evil in his eyes? You struck down Uriah the Hittite with the sword and took his wife to be your own. You killed him with the sword of the Ammonites."
—II Samuel 12:6-9, NIV

"Then David said to Nathan, "I have sinned against the Lord." Nathan replied, "The Lord has taken away your sin. You are not going to die. David noticed that his attendants were whispering among themselves, and he realized the child was dead. "Is the child dead?" he asked. "Yes," they replied, "he is dead." Then David got up from the ground. After he had washed, put on lotions and changed his clothes, he went into the house of the Lord and worshiped. Then he went to his own house, and at his request they served him food, and he ate."
—II Samuel 12:13, 19, 20, NIV

Errors, whether intentional or not, will always occur, and leaders are not exempt. David had committed the sins of covetousness, adultery, and murder. God, understandably displeased, sent Prophet Nathan.

Nathan, using a proverb, asked the King what should be done to a man who committed such sins. David, burning with anger, responded without hesitation that such a man must pay a huge price, showing no pity. Then, Nathan revealed that David was that man.

Nathan reminded David of his humble origin and current station, highlighting how he could have had anything, yet despised the word of the Lord by committing evil.

Here's the gem: leaders understand that God chastises those He loves. Like David, they quickly repent. Instead of arguing, David confessed to Nathan, "I have sinned against the Lord." Nathan replied, "The Lord has taken away your sins," although consequences remained.

David faced punishment for his actions, but this shouldn't discourage Godly leaders from owning up to mistakes and repenting to be restored. As a leader, be quick to repent of your sins; never let pride overtake you.

- 🛡 129 -

DANGEROUS SUPERIOR ARGUMENT

"The woman said, "Why then have you devised a thing like this against the people of God? When the king says this, does he not convict himself, for the king has not brought back his banished son? Like water spilled on the ground, which cannot be recovered, so we must die. But that is not what God desires; rather, he devises ways so that a banished person does not remain banished from him."
—*II Samuel 14:13, 14, NIV*

Leaders often face varied viewpoints and opinions, making judgment calls based on available information. Even wise leaders may succumb to what I term "dangerous superior arguments," which can be persuasive but harmful.

Joab, David's General, knew that the King longed for his son Absalom, who had committed a grave sin by carrying out revenge on his half-brother Amnon for raping his sister Tamar, who lived as a desolate woman. For two years, Absalom plotted his reaction. When it seemed all was forgotten, he called for a banquet for all the king's sons and the King and his attendants. (His future actions of betrayal may reveal that he probably wanted to take out the entire royal house in one clean swoop.) He informed his men that when Amnon was high on wine, he should be struck down. After doing this, his real intention was revealed, and he fled to Geshur, where he lived for three years.

Joab, realizing that David missed his son, would ask for a wise woman to appear before the King and put words in her mouth. Having boxed the King into a corner, where he himself admitted his folly, she would ask him why he had devised such a thing and not brought back his banished son. She reminded him, "Like water that is spilled on the ground, which cannot be recovered, all must die, and that even God Himself devises ways so that a banished person does not remain banished from Him."

David would bow to this superior argument, and after establishing the source of the wisdom as Joab, instructed him to go and bring back the young man Absalom. However, with the proviso that he must go to his own house and not see his face, which, after a short while, and pressurizing Joab, he would once again be reunited. Though briefly, before unleashing on his father a coup to take over the kingdom for himself and sending his father on a forced exile.

The gem here is for leaders to be wary of intelligent and superior arguments, though sensible, can bring a leader's ruin. If David knew that despite forgiving Absalom, the prince would still go on to cause him more harm, he probably would have left him in exile. Godly leaders must be wary of viewpoints which seem harmless but carry within them potentially dangerous seeds of destruction.

- 💠 130 -

WEARY OF CONSPIRACY

"And Absalom would add, "If only I were appointed judge in the land! Then everyone who has a complaint or case could come to me and I would see that they receive justice." Absalom behaved in this way toward all the Israelites who came to the king asking for justice, and so he stole the hearts of the people of Israel."
—II Samuel 15:4, 6, NIV

Absalom was clearly back in the scheme of things, having regained his father King David's favor, who remained oblivious to the four years of scheming and planning a coup to destroy him. Perhaps Absalom's motivations stemmed from David's inaction after his sister Tamar's rape or a simple desire to be King.

David failed to recognize the conspiracy unfolding under his own roof. Otherwise, he would have detected the smell of betrayal in his palace's hallways.

Over time, Absalom acquired a chariot worthy of a king and assembled an advance party of fifty men. He rose early, attending to the complaints of people who had come to see his father and judge matters. Showing humility to all, Absalom stole the hearts of Israel's people.

Surprisingly, David remained unaware until Absalom

requested to worship God in Hebron, knowing his father would accept. Seizing the opportunity, Absalom declared his kingship, winning over notable supporters, including Ahithophel, David's counselor. The conspiracy gained strength, and Absalom's following grew.

The coup reached its climax when David discovered that the people's hearts were with Absalom. To avoid bloodshed, he fled the city with his household, leaving ten concubines to tend to the palace. David departed, weeping, upon hearing of various betrayals, uncertain if he would ever return to the city that bore his name.

Godly leaders must beware of conspiracies; they are real and can spread like cancer if unattended. Leaders must keep their eyes open and ears alert, not obsessively, but with wisdom, recognizing that greater positions attract greater opposition.

The gem here is: Godly leaders must understand that spiritual and human conspiracies will challenge their leadership. Be wise, spot them early, and quash them to avoid exile, as David was forced to undertake.

- 〇 131 -

THE COUNSEL OF A LEADER

"Now in those days the advice Ahithophel gave was like that of one who inquires of God. That was how both David and Absalom regarded all of Ahithophel's advice."
—*II Samuel 16:23, NIV*

"Now David had been told, "Ahithophel is among the conspirators with Absalom." So David prayed, "Lord, turn Ahithophel's counsel into foolishness." When David arrived at the summit, where people used to worship God, Hushai the Arkite was there to meet him, his robe torn and dust on his head. David said to him, "If you go with me, you will be a burden to me. But if you return to the city and say to Absalom, 'Your Majesty, I will be your servant; I was your father's servant in the past, but now I will be your servant,' then you can help me by frustrating Ahithophel's advice. Won't the priests Zadok and Abiathar be there with you? Tell them anything you hear in the king's palace."
—*II Samuel 15: 31 -37, NIV*

The markings of any great leader are the quality of counsel they receive during their tenure, and David was no exception. Every leader has blind spots and needs unbiased minds to provide wisdom on specific actions. A counselor can bring great peace or reproach to a leader.

Ahitophel's advice sustained David's leadership, his words were so wise they seemed prophetic. Scholars offer divergent reasons for Ahitophel's allegiance switch, but David understood the power of his counsel and prayed it would be turned to foolishness.

Recognizing counsel's importance, David instructed Hushai, his confidant, to return to Jerusalem and frustrate Ahitophel's plans.

Ahitophel's counsel to Absalom demonstrated its power. First, he advised Absalom to publicly sleep with David's concubines on the rooftop, effectively severing reconciliation paths with David. Second, he suggested pursuing David relentlessly with 12,000 men, capitalizing on David's weakness.

Although Hushai countered Ahitophel's advice, God intended to frustrate it, leading to Absalom's downfall. Ignoring Ahitophel's counsel would lead to the advisors depression and his eventual suicide.

Godly leaders understand the critical gem that the counsel they receive is vital. Ultimately, Hushai's counsel led to him letting David slip out of his grasp, and eventually Absalom's own death. Leaders must wisely and contemplatively choose who has their ear. Ahitophel's motive was likely ambition for personal power, and he had a reputation for practical sagacity. Though he didn't reveal his intentions early, his influence was evident in managing the new king's affairs.

- 🛡 132 -

PINCH OF SALT

"David then said to Abishai and all his officials, "My son, my own flesh and blood, is trying to kill me. How much more, then, this Benjamite! Leave him alone; let him curse, for the Lord has told him to. It may be that the Lord will look upon my misery and restore to me his covenant blessing instead of his curse today."
—II Samuel 16:11-12 NIV

There are things that a leader must learn to take with a pinch of salt, not everything demands full attention at the exact moment. David, during his march out of Jerusalem, approached Bahurim, where Shimei, son of Gera, from Saul's clan, cursed him, pelting David and his entourage with stones despite the heavy military presence.

Shimei accused David of being a murderer and scoundrel. When Abishai, son of Zeruiah, asked to deliver Shimei's head to the King, David responded, "If my own son seeks to kill me, why not this Benjamite? Let him curse, for the Lord has told him to. Perhaps the Lord will see my misery and repay me with good for the cursing I receive today." David understood he had bigger priorities than one troublesome individual. He took the matter with a pinch of salt, recognizing a leader cannot allocate all their attention to every issue.

The gem here is: Godly leaders understand the critical allocation of their attention. Otherwise, they may waste energy on trivial matters. Be wise, handling some issues with the same finesse masterful cooks handle meal preparations – with a pinch of salt.

- ⛉ 133 -

KNOW YOUR LEADERSHIP WORTH

"But the men said, "You must not go out; if we are forced to flee, they won't care about us. Even if half of us die, they won't care; but you are worth ten thousand of us. It would be better now for you to give us support from the city." The king answered, "I will do whatever seems best to you." So the king stood beside the gate while all his men marched out in units of hundreds and of thousands."
—II Samuel 18:3, 4, NIV

Understanding your leadership worth is critical. Many leaders often forget this important point: your presence cannot be everywhere, and your time is equally critical.

David mustered the men with him, appointing commanders of thousands and hundreds, and announced his intention to march out with them. However, they rejected their King's advice, citing his leadership worth:

"You must not go out. If we flee, our enemies won't care, and even if half of us die, no one will care. But you, David, are worth ten thousand of us. It's better if you support us from the city."

David replied, "Do what seems best." He stood by the gate, waving his army off to battle.

A leader who fails to build their worth before those they lead will soon become worthless. Leadership worth must be measurable by both the leader and their followers.

Leadership worth determines where human and material resources are directed. Ignoring this may make a leader a cheap commodity.

The gem here is: build worth that others will lay everything down to protect, recognizing that your loss is too great a sacrifice.

The men knew David's death had far-reaching repercussions and that he should sit out this battle.

A leader must know, build, acknowledge, and protect their worth at all times.

- 🛡 134 -

ONE HEART AND SOUL
AND MIND WITH FOLLOWERS

"Then Joab went into the house to the king and said, "Today you have humiliated all your men, who have just saved your life and the lives of your sons and daughters and the lives of your wives and concubines. You love those who hate you and hate those who love you. You have made it clear today that the commanders and their men mean nothing to you. I see that you would be pleased if Absalom were alive today and all of us were dead. Now go out and encourage your men. I swear by the Lord that if you don't go out, not a man will be left with you by nightfall. This will be worse for you than all the calamities that have come on you from your youth till now." So the king got up and took his seat in the gateway. When the men were told, "The king is sitting in the gateway," they all came before him. Meanwhile, the Israelites had fled to their homes."
—II Samuel 19:5-8, NIV

When King David's army marched out to face Absalom's army, David commanded his generals, Joab, Abishai, and Ittai, to spare his son for his sake. All the troops heard the king's orders.

David's army routed Israel's, resulting in 20,000 casualties. The forest claimed more lives than the sword. Absalom, riding a mule, got his hair entangled in a large oak's branches and hung in mid-air. A soldier informed Joab, who scolded him for not striking Absalom down.

The soldier reminded Joab of the king's orders, but Joab ignored him and killed Absalom with three javelins. Ten armor-bearers surrounded and struck him until he died. His remains were thrown into a forest pit, covered with a huge pile of thrones.

David, informed of Absalom's death, wept in the room above the gate. Joab told him he had humiliated his soldiers, pointing out that 20,000 men had fought to reclaim the kingdom, and David's mourning seemed to value Absalom's life over theirs.

Joab warned David of potential mutiny and advised him to encourage the men. David, recognizing Joab's wisdom, rose and sat in the gateway, receiving his soldiers.

The gem here is: Godly leaders must connect with their followers, being one heart and soul. Losing this connection risks losing everything.

David's son's death was painful, but he needed to prioritize his soldiers' feelings. A cardinal principle of leadership is that followers want to know their leader cares. Godly leaders must be one with their followers, showing appreciation and encouragement.

- 135 -

VOTE OF CONFIDENCE

*"He won over the hearts of the men of Judah so that
they were all of one mind. They sent word to the king,
"Return, you and all your men."*
—II Samuel 19:14, NIV

After Absalom's veil was lifted, the people seemed to recall King David's past achievements: delivering them from enemies and rescuing them from the Philistines. A general vote of confidence ensued.

David sent word to Judah, asking why they shouldn't lead the way in his return. Winning others' confidence is challenging, but achievable when hearts and minds are won over.

Like David, the people initiated his return, with tribes sending thousands to meet him at the Jordan River. David didn't rush back to the throne until certain of his acceptance. The gem here is: leaders must establish acceptance among their followers. Failure to do so results in leading people without unity of mind and heart.

A ruler without a vote of confidence will see their leadership erode. David's cautious approach ensured a strong foundation for his renewed leadership.

- 136 -

LEARNING FROM PAST TREACHERY

"Now a troublemaker named Sheba son of Bikri, a Benjamite, happened to be there. He sounded the trumpet and shouted, "We have no share in David, no part in Jesse's son! Every man to his tent, Israel!" So all the men of Israel deserted David to follow Sheba son of Bikri. But the men of Judah stayed by their king all the way from the Jordan to Jerusalem. David said to Abishai, "Now Sheba son of Bikri will do us more harm than Absalom did. Take your master's men and pursue him, or he will find fortified cities and escape from us." That is not the case. A man named Sheba son of Bikri, from the hill country of Ephraim, has lifted up his hand against the king, against David. Hand over this one man, and I'll withdraw from the city." The woman said to Joab, "His head will be thrown to you from the wall." Then the woman went to all the people with her wise advice, and they cut off the head of Sheba son of Bikri and threw it to Joab. So he sounded the trumpet, and his men dispersed from the city, each returning to his home. And Joab went back to the king in Jerusalem."
—II Samuel 20:1-22, NIV

Wise leaders learn from the past, especially lessons from past treachery. Returning from exile after Absalom's conspiracy and death, King David faced another challenge. As he crossed into Gilgal, the men of Israel asked why Judah had "stolen" the king away. Judah replied that their kinship with David justified their actions. Israel countered, claiming ten shares in the king and greater claim, accusing Judah of contempt.

Amidst this argument, the troublemaker Sheba, a Benjamite, sounded a trumpet and shouted, "We have no share in David, no part in Jesse's son! Every man to his tent!" Israel deserted David, following Sheba.

David, seasoned by past experiences, recognized the danger. He told Abishai that Sheba would cause more harm than Absalom and instructed him to pursue Sheba before he entered a fortified city.

Sheba traversed several regions until he was cornered in Abel Beth Maacah. As Joab's men battered the walls, a wise woman intervened, promising Sheba's head in exchange for withdrawal. Sheba was beheaded, and his head thrown to Joab, who sounded the trumpet, dispersing his men.

The gem here is: Godly leaders must prevent past treachery from repeating itself. Like David, learn from past experiences and recognize similar traits in others. Though the circumstances may differ, the poisonous fruit remains the same.

- 137 -

SOLUTION OF THE PRESENT CAN BE FOUND IN THE PAST

"During the reign of David, there was a famine for three successive years; so David sought the face of the Lord. The Lord said, "It is on account of Saul and his blood-stained house; it is because he put the Gibeonites to death." The king summoned the Gibeonites and spoke to them. (Now the Gibeonites were not a part of Israel but were survivors of the Amorites; the Israelites had sworn to spare them, but Saul in his zeal for Israel and Judah had tried to annihilate them.) David asked the Gibeonites, "What shall I do for you? How shall I make atonement so that you will bless the Lord's inheritance?" The Gibeonites answered him, "We have no right to demand silver or gold from Saul or his family, nor do we have the right to put anyone in Israel to death." "What do you want me to do for you?" David asked. They answered the king, "As for the man who destroyed us and plotted against us so that we have been decimated and have no place anywhere in Israel, let seven of his male descendants be given to us to be killed and their bodies exposed before the Lord at Gibeah of Saul—the Lord's chosen one." So the king said, "I will give them to you." They buried the bones of Saul and his son Jonathan in the tomb of Saul's father Kish, at Zela in Benjamin, and did everything the king commanded. After that, God answered prayer in behalf of the land."
—II Samuel 21:1-6, 14, NIV

Throughout this book, we've emphasized that leaders face unpalatable situations requiring unusual wisdom. Many leaders frantically search for solutions, but sometimes, Godly wisdom reveals answers in the past.

During David's reign, a severe famine lasted three years. David sought God's face, inquiring why his people suffered. The answer lay in the past: King Saul's house had slain the Gibeonites and Amorites who were protected by a vow.

David initiated reconciliation, asking the Gibeonites how to compensate for the injustice. They requested no riches or individual's head, being strangers in the land. Prompted by David, they asked for seven male descendants of Saul to be killed and exposed.

David agreed, sparing Mephibosheth but killing all of (Saul's) concubines children and subsequently, David retrieved Saul and Jonathan's bodies from Jabesh Gilead and buried them in Benjamin. Then, God answered prayer, and the famine ceased.

The gem here is: leaders must humble themselves to seek solutions from the past. Much is buried and covered by predecessors' actions.

Effective leaders recognize the value of understanding past mistakes and injustices, using this knowledge to guide their decisions and bring resolution.

- 🛡 138 -

RIGHTEOUSNESS & FEAR OF GOD

"The Spirit of the Lord spoke through me; his word was on my tongue. The God of Israel spoke, the Rock of Israel said to me: 'When one rules over people in righteousness, when he rules in the fear of God, he is like the light of morning at sunrise on a cloudless morning, like the brightness after rain that brings grass from the earth."
—II Samuel 23:2-4, NIV

On his death bed, King David inspired by the spirit of God, who spoke through him and with the inspired words rolling off his tongue he reminded leaders of what is essential based on what God said to him, now I must emphasize this is directly from the mouth of the creator, he stressed that when a leader rules over people in righteousness and rules in the fear of God, he likened such individuals to be like the light of morning at sunrise and the brightness after rain that causes the grass of the earth to flourish.

The dual qualities were righteousness and possessing a fear of God, these qualities in the life of a leader, God equates with elements of his creation, we all know how after a rough night we look forward to the light of the morning or maybe after a serious storm the brightness that manifests to cover the gloom, weariness and drab feelings such a weather brings.

The Gem here is that leaders must be righteous and have the fear of God and they will be the kind of leaders the people eagerly look forward to and are grateful for.

- 🛡 139 -

LEADER-RAISE MEN

"During harvest time, three of the thirty chief warriors came down to David at the cave of Adullam, while a band of Philistines was encamped in the Valley of Rephaim. At that time David was in the stronghold, and the Philistine garrison was at Bethlehem. David longed for water and said, "Oh, that someone would get me a drink of water from the well near the gate of Bethlehem!" So the three mighty warriors broke through the Philistine lines, drew water from the well near the gate of Bethlehem and carried it back to David. But he refused to drink it; instead, he poured it out before the Lord. "Far be it from me, Lord, to do this!" he said. "Is it not the blood of men who went at the risk of their lives?" And David would not drink it. Such were the exploits of the three mighty warriors."
—II Samuel 23:13-17, NIV

Thirty-seven men were the total number that David raised. 2 Samuel 23 is a testament to the exploits of these men, who were called David's mighty warriors. From using a spear to kill eight hundred men to another having his hand frozen to his sword, to defending territories, these men could be likened to our modern-day fictional superheroes. All this was a result of David's intentional effort in raising men.

The most inspiring account was when, during harvest time, three of the thirty chief warriors came to David at the cave of Adullam. Meanwhile, a band of Philistines were encamped in the Valley of Rephaim, and at that time, David was in the stronghold, while the enemy garrison was at Bethlehem. David longed for water from the well near the gate of Bethlehem, and the three mighty warriors went on a daring mission, breaking through enemy lines to draw water and carrying it back to David. He, understanding deeper spiritual realities, refused to drink it, likening it to the blood of the men who risked everything to satisfy the thirst of their King.

Leaders must understand that, while serving people, their other responsibility is raising men. Those are the real testament of a leader; his badge of honor lies in the men he raised while leading. This should be a conscious goal of every leader.

The Gem here is that leaders understand that when the curtain drops, what truly outlives leaders are not monuments or works of their hands, though noble, but what truly outlives them are the men they invested in while leading. Therefore, like David, you must embark on raising your own mighty men who will stand to uphold you and ensure your legacy is timeless.

- 💎 140 -

PRIDE

> *"Again the anger of the Lord burned against Israel, and he incited David against them, saying, "Go and take a census of Israel and Judah." David was conscience-stricken after he had counted the fighting men, and he said to the Lord, "I have sinned greatly in what I have done. Now, Lord, I beg you, take away the guilt of your servant. I have done a very foolish thing."*
> —II Samuel 24:1, 10, NIV

When the Lord's anger burned against Israel, He incited David to manifest pride, the arch-nemesis of a leader.

The victories wrought by the Israeli army were not just a matter of numerical advantage or strategic military models. Right from when they left Egypt to the present day, they had fought countless wars and celebrated unexplained victories due to the hand of God in the scheme of their affairs. Thus, counting the army was seen as a means of taking pride in numbers rather than in God.

When David told Joab and the army commanders to take a census of Israel and Judah and enroll the fighting men, so he might know how many they were, even the commanders complained about the foolishness of this endeavor. However, he overruled them. After nine months and twenty days, they reported to the King:

800,000 able-bodied men in Israel

500,000 in Judah

The reality dawned on him; when his conscience was stricken, he said to God, "I have committed a major sin." He begged for the guilt to be taken away.

The result of his ingratitude and pride was a multiple-choice option given to him by God via the prophet Gad. He was offered three alternatives:

Three years of famine

Three months fleeing from his enemies while being pursued

Three days of plague in the land

David, understanding God's benevolence, chose to fall into God's hands. A plague came upon the land, costing 70,000 lives, until the Lord relented and stopped the angel from striking more people.
Godly leaders, flee from any action of pride. Avoid anything that removes God as the epicenter of all your decisions.

The Gem here is that leaders must never get ahead of themselves and allow disaster to be visited on those they lead because of pride; it is too high a price to pay.

- ◍ 141 -

PRICE

"But the king replied to Araunah, "No, I insist on paying you for it. I will not sacrifice to the Lord my God burnt offerings that cost me nothing." So David bought the threshing floor and the oxen and paid fifty shekels of silver for them. David built an altar to the Lord there and sacrificed burnt offerings and fellowship offerings. Then the Lord answered his prayer in behalf of the land, and the plague on Israel was stopped."
—II Samuel 24:24, 25, NIV

A leader's walk involves making decisions with far-reaching consequences. Previously, we saw King David's pride lead to God permitting a plague on his people. As an act of mercy, God instructed the angel to withdraw, and David saw the angel at Araunah the Jebusite's threshing floor.

Gad instructed David to build an altar there. When David offered to buy the threshing floor to stop the plague, Araunah generously offered everything, including oxen, sledges, and ox yokes for wood.

However, David, demonstrating his leadership and Godly values, refused to accept the offer without payment. He emphasized that he wouldn't sacrifice to God anything that cost him nothing.

As a leader, David understood the importance of paying a price to attract God's intervention. This principle remains crucial for leaders: nothing is too great or too good to give to God.

The Gem here is: Godly leaders must be willing to pay a price for God's intervention in their affairs, recognizing that true sacrifice is essential for divine blessings.

THE BOOK OF
I KINGS

- ⬡ 142 -

WHEN SILENCE IS NOT GOLDEN

"Now Adonijah, whose mother was Haggith, put himself forward and said, "I will be king." So he got chariots and horses ready, with fifty men to run ahead of him. (His father had never rebuked him by asking, "Why do you behave as you do?" He was also very handsome and was born next after Absalom.)"
—*I Kings 1:5-6, NIV*

There is a popular phrase about silence being golden, but leaders must understand that this is not fully applicable to them. There is a time to be quiet and a time when your voice must be heard.

King David was already very old; in fact, so old that clothing could no longer keep him warm, and a young virgin was sought to carry out the task. Interestingly, lightning does strike twice in the same place. Many years before, Absalom had done the same act of attributing men and chariots to himself before hatching his plan, and his half-brother, Adonijah, would borrow a page from the same book by getting chariots and horses ready, with fifty men running ahead of him.

What is most important to note is that the Bible records that David made the same mistake again; he never rebuked him by saying anything or asked why he was behaving in such a reckless and outlandish manner. Often, silence may be interpreted as a subtle endorsement of an action, and it clearly seems the children of the King understood and rode on this to commit what may have been branded treacherous acts against the throne.

Even David's most trusted allies, like Joab the General and Abiathar the priest, gave him their support without seeking confirmation on his choice of successor.

The Gem what Godly leaders must appreciate here is that they must apply wisdom in all matters, but specifically when they should speak, they should not be silent. They should be bold to rebuke anybody who is capable of creating division and rancor by their acts or omission. Silence is golden, but other times it must be uttered for all to hear your stand and position on critical matters.

- ◉ 143 -

SUCCESSOR

"My Lord the king, the eyes of all Israel are on you, to learn from you who will sit on the throne of my Lord the king after him. Otherwise, as soon as my Lord the king is laid to rest with his ancestors, I and my son Solomon will be treated as criminals." Is this something my Lord the king has done without letting his servants know who should sit on the throne of my Lord the king after him?"
—I Kings 1:20, 21- 27, NIV

"Then King David said, "Call in Bathsheba." So she came into the king's presence and stood before him. The king then took an oath: "As surely as the Lord lives, who has delivered me out of every trouble, I will surely carry out this very day what I swore to you by the Lord, the God of Israel: Solomon your son shall be king after me, and he will sit on my throne in my place."
—I Kings 1:28-30, NIV

The touchy subject matter of succession is one that has plagued leaders of all ages from time immemorial. Who is the right person to take the reins of power? Who is the right choice to uphold the ideals and vision of the leader they would succeed? Now, depending on the setup, like in a democracy where the choice is by the people, but in other settings, we find that the outgoing leader, whether stated or not, has a huge part and strong influence on who succeeds them.

David understood that if he did not act in a clear manner, his Kingdom would be in disarray after his demise, and his family torn apart. When informed of Adonijah's actions, Bathsheba, to whom he had promised that her son would take over—and probably mentioned it to a few others—approached him with great fear about what would be the outcome if he suddenly slept with his fathers without appointing a successor. She emphasized something that all leaders must always consider: who will lead after you?

David, realizing what would befall his legacy, was quick to take an oath before Bathsheba and Nathan the prophet on his choice of Solomon. (Another assumption is that David, being a spiritual man and a good shepherd, would have sought God before handing over his people to Solomon).

The Gem here is that Godly leaders don't sit idly watching others fight for the soul of their organization or kingdom. When permissible, they make a public statement or take a stand based on their experience and conviction on who the right person is to take over.

- ◌ 144 -

ROUTING OUT THE OPPOSITION

"Then the king gave the order to Benaiah son of Jehoiada, and he went out and struck Shimei down and he died. The kingdom was now established in Solomon's hands."
—I Kings 2:46, NIV

Solomon, the chosen, now sat on his father's throne, who with his final words gave his son strategic moves to be undertaken, which included routing out opposition to his rule, individuals who at one point in time or the other had shown their hand, making governance untenable for the late King.

It is therefore no surprise that Solomon had peace like no other King in Israel, beyond his wisdom; David ensured that there were no enemies lurking around the royal hallways. The instruction was to get rid of his long faithful ally Joab because he shed blood in peace time, and to Shimei, who rained bitter curses on him, he was expected to deal with them according to wisdom.

The Gem here is that Godly leaders must understand that one of their first action points is to isolate those who will be in opposition for a smooth reign. Do not ignore or run with the assumption that leopards can change their spots or zebras their stripes; many of those who opposed your predecessor will likely visit you with the same hostility if given the right time and opportunity.

- ⬙ 145 -

WISDOM TO LEAD

"So give your servant a discerning heart to govern your people and to distinguish between right and wrong. For who is able to govern this great people of yours?"
—I Kings 3:9, NIV

"When all Israel heard the verdict the king had given, they held the king in awe, because they saw that he had wisdom from God to administer justice."
—I Kings 3:28, NIV

"God gave Solomon wisdom and very great insight, and a breadth of understanding as measureless as the sand on the seashore. Solomon's wisdom was greater than the wisdom of all the people of the East, and greater than all the wisdom of Egypt."
—I Kings 4:29, 30, NIV

Can wisdom ever fully be over-emphasized? King Solomon had shown his devotion to the Lord by walking according to the instructions given by his father. He went to offer sacrifices at Gibeon, a thousand burnt offerings, and that night the Lord appeared to him, offering a blank cheque for the young King to fill.

Solomon won the heart of God with his response, asking for what every leader requires to lead, regardless of the occasion: Wisdom. He made a passionate case, requesting a discerning heart to govern God's people and to distinguish between right and wrong. The Lord was so pleased that He responded, "Since you did not ask for long life, wealth, or the death of your enemies, but only discernment in administering justice, you will have wisdom, and all that you did not ask for."

Subsequently, the famous tale of the two women laying claim to one baby would be the test of this wisdom. After Solomon gave his wise ruling, it is said that when all of Israel heard the verdict, they held him in awe because it was evident he had wisdom from God to administer justice. This wisdom was also evident in the selection and makeup of his cabinet. The caliber of personalities assembled clearly made ruling easier. He had so much wisdom, and his breadth of understanding was as measureless as the sand on the seashore, surpassing the wisdom of all the people of the east and Egypt.

There is hardly any Godly leader who can be effective in leading others without the presence of wisdom. It is a difficult task that will make such an experience a burden rather than a delight. Leaders, especially in this dispensation, must tirelessly seek wisdom to administer justice in a way that is pleasing to God and also attract prosperity to their areas of operation.

The gem here is that Godly leaders must understand that wisdom is the fuel needed for the operation of their leadership vehicle. To lead themselves and others, wisdom is essential and cannot be dispensed with.

- ◎ 146 -

LEADERSHIP CADRE

> *"So King Solomon ruled over all Israel. And these were his chief officials: Azariah son of Zadok—the priest; Elihoreph and Ahijah, sons of Shisha—secretaries; Jehoshaphat son of Ahilud—recorder; Benaiah son of Jehoiada—commander in chief; Zadok and Abiathar—priests; Azariah son of Nathan—in charge of the district governors; Zabud son of Nathan—a priest and adviser to the king; Ahishar—palace administrator; Adoniram son of Abda—in charge of forced labor. Solomon had twelve district governors over all Israel, who supplied provisions for the king and the royal household. Each one had to provide supplies for one month in the year."*
> —I Kings 4:1-7, NIV

I am a personal fan of structure and system in the operation of leadership, for one major fact: no man can do it all by himself, no matter how wise, talented, or proficient. You need others who you will delegate responsibilities to, to carry out acts in your name, and this was a gem that King Solomon embraced.

In the opening years of his rule, we see him establish a competent leadership cadre, an organogram of how power flowed and where responsibilities were domiciled. He created structures that covered vital areas that his leadership required, from spiritual matters where Azariah served, to his appointment of a secretary to his cabinet showing his desire for order, to Jehoshaphat responsible for recording all official matters, to Benaiah who helped him become King and was one of David's mighty men, given the role of commander in chief, to Azariah overseeing the district governors, Zabud a priest and adviser, Ahishar handling the role of Chief of Staff or palace administrator, to Adoniram in charge of forced labor, and finally the appointment of twelve district governors over all Israel who were in charge of supplying provisions to the royal household.

It was a well-oiled machine that could only guarantee results.

Godly leaders must understand the need to have a leadership team in place if the position demands such. Burning out is a reality that exists among leaders, and embracing this gem will ensure you have not only other shoulders to lift heavy loads but diverse opinions and viewpoints to consider when making decisions.

The gem here is that Godly leaders must understand the need to have a leadership team in place.

- ◍ 147 -

YOUR LEGACY IS A HIGHWAY OTHERS WILL TRAVEL ON

"When Hiram king of Tyre heard that Solomon had been anointed king to succeed his father David, he sent his envoys to Solomon, because he had always been on friendly terms with David."
—I Kings 5:1, NIV

We have on several occasions already emphasized the importance of legacy, but it won't hurt to mention it again. Legacy is the one thing, apart from men, that will outlive your leadership.

King David was a very strategic King who built a legacy that outlived him and favored his successor. When Hiram, the King of Tyre, heard that Solomon had been anointed king, he immediately sent his envoys to Solomon for the sole reason that he had always been on friendly terms with his father.

There are many leaders whose actions make it near impossible for those coming after to ride on the highway they have built to enjoy any benefits. Many leaders, unfortunately, carried away by the glamour of leading, engage in bridge-burning, forgetting that power, like all things in this realm, is transient. Their actions will remain even after they have been long forgotten.

Godly leaders must do differently by ensuring they build bridges that others can enjoy traveling on, not ones that will be avoided. It is a duty of care owed to the future.

The gem here is that Godly leaders must prioritize building a lasting, beneficial legacy that will outlive their leadership.

- ◌ 148 -

ALLIANCES FOR COMMON GOOD

"The Lord gave Solomon wisdom, just as he had promised him. There were peaceful relations between Hiram and Solomon, and the two of them made a treaty."
—I Kings 5:12, NIV

Wise leaders build alliances, understanding that the world's structure is one of interdependence. No individual or kingdom has the sole preserve of having everything, and for that singular reason, there is a need for others to take what we have and give us things we don't possess, also for the sake of peace.

This is the place for alliances between leaders. Godly leaders must never tire of seeking new alliances to build peaceful relations. Today, we see many nations entering into treaties to guarantee their peaceful existence and economic sustenance, all possible only through the vision and boldness of a leader.

As a leader, you must build associations for mutual benefit—relationships based on similarity of interests, nature, or qualities. However, be wary of unholy alliances that will defy and overshadow your leadership. Many negative alliances lead to ruin due to compromise and negative influence.

God expressly forbade the Israelites from alliances with the inhabitants of the promised land, knowing such would deflect them from Him. Human tendency is to manifest traits and qualities of those you are yoked to, either for good or bad.

The gem here is that alliances can lead to great prosperity for those you lead, when leaders are prayerfully guided on who to associate with.

- ◉ 149 -

INTEGRITY AND UPRIGHTNESS

"As for you, if you walk before me faithfully with integrity of heart and uprightness, as David your father did, and do all I command and observe my decrees and laws, I will establish your royal throne over Israel forever, as I promised David your father when I said, 'You shall never fail to have a successor on the throne of Israel."
—I Kings 9:4, 5, NIV

"Whoever walks in integrity walks securely, but whoever takes crooked paths will be found out."
—Proverbs 10:9-11, NIV

Integrity is the quality of being honest and having strong moral principles, or better still, the state of being whole and undivided. Its etymology reveals its origin from the word "integer," meaning a number with no decimal or fractional part. In other words, what you see is what you get.

God places great importance on integrity in His leaders. Speaking to King Solomon, He extolled the virtues of his father David, consciously mentioning what made him a favorite: "He walked before Me faithfully and with integrity of heart and uprightness." For this reason, David was given an eternal lamp of remembrance burning before God, ensuring he would always have a successor on the throne of Israel.

Leadership and integrity should be inseparable, but unfortunately, many leaders have severed the ties. We find many called to lead who lack moral principles and are void of honesty.

In the book of Proverbs, we see that "whoever walks in integrity is secure." They don't fear discovery, constant looking over their shoulder, or apprehension at every accusation. They can face whatever is thrown at them.

Jesus Christ embodied integrity, and it's expected that we model Him by ensuring our lives as leaders become a living and breathing version of Scripture.

The gem here is that Godly leaders uphold the virtues of integrity and uprightness, and no earthly riches or treasure will make them trade it in.

- ◻ 150 -

PROJECT MANAGEMENT

"But Solomon did not make slaves of any of the Israelites; they were his fighting men, his government officials, his officers, his captains, and the commanders of his chariots and charioteers. They were also the chief officials in charge of Solomon's projects—550 officials supervising those who did the work."
—*I Kings 9:22, 23, NIV*

Leadership also means eyes on the ball, fixation on the prize. One of the reasons many leaders fail is due to failure to supervise. Solomon was a builder due to the blood-stained hands of his father who couldn't embark on the building of the project. Solomon ensured that he had chief officials who were in charge of projects only, the Bible recognizes that they were five hundred and fifty in number, quite a sizable number.

Project management is the application of processes, methods, skills, knowledge, and experience to achieve specific objectives. A leader's role is also primarily one of project management, of individuals and resources, often such projects can be gigantic in size and operation, thereby making it almost humanly impossible for such an individual to cover all bases and like we begun this gem drop the ball. Solomon must have had concurrent projects, the most tasking would have been building a temple that is befitting to God, according to his standard. No leader can escape from managing and supervising projects and why it is important you employ the strategy of having competent managers who can manage on a macro and micro level to ensure performance and adherence to quality standards.

The Gem for Godly leaders is not to undermine the importance of project management so as to hit set target.

- ◻ 151 -

IMPORTANCE OF EXPANSION

"King Solomon also built ships at Ezion Geber, which is near Elath in Edom, on the shore of the Red Sea. And Hiram sent his men—sailors who knew the sea— to serve in the fleet with Solomon's men. They sailed to Ophir and brought back 420 talents of gold, which they delivered to King Solomon."
—*I Kings 9:26-28, NIV*

Leaders must work on growth and expansion to ensure that they don't lead in a stunted environment. King Solomon understood this gem and was not content with the status quo, he was concerned about the prosperity of his people and one of the things he did was to build ships on the shore of the Red Sea, and with the previously mentioned alliance, Hiram sent him men who knew the sea to serve in the fleet and it is on record that they sailed far to Ophir and brought back 420 Talents of Gold.

He was involved in so many economic activities that caused silver and gold to be common in Israel. A leader's hunger must be for growth and this must never be taken for granted.

The Gem here for Godly leaders is that it is important to expand in leaps and bounds, prosperity makes it easier for those being led to stay loyal, you would discover that in the absence of growth and expansion, such a leader is sitting on a ticking time bomb, that will surely go off at an unexpected moment when the patience of those following run thin.

- ◻ 152 -

REWARD FOR PREPARATION

"When the queen of Sheba saw all the wisdom of Solomon and the palace he had built, the food on his table, the seating of his officials, the attending servants in their robes, his cupbearers, and the burnt offerings he made at the temple of the Lord, she was over-whelmed. She said to the king, "The report I heard in my own country about your achievements and your wisdom is true. But I did not believe these things until I came and saw with my own eyes. Indeed, not even half was told me; in wisdom and wealth you have far exceeded the report I heard. How happy your people must be! How happy your officials, who continually stand before you and hear your wisdom! Praise be to the Lord your God, who has delighted in you and placed you on the throne of Israel. Because of the Lord's eternal love for Israel, he has made you king to maintain justice and righteousness." And she gave the king 120 talents of gold, large quantities of spices, and precious stones. Never again were so many spices brought in as those the queen of Sheba gave to King Solomon."
—I Kings 10:4-10, NIV

There are fewer things in the world that offer such a rewarding return on investment as preparation. King Solomon, one of the most learned kings, applied himself to gathering knowledge and applied it to his surroundings, reaping huge rewards.

Queen Sheba, having heard of Solomon's wisdom, traveled from Ethiopia to Israel, carrying great spices and treasures to verify the legend. But she didn't meet just any man; she encountered a leader who had invested in mental transformation, holding value for all who interacted with him.

The Queen witnessed Solomon's wisdom, palace, exquisite cuisine, servants' attire, and burnt offerings, leaving her overwhelmed. She acknowledged that what she had heard was only half of what she witnessed, exceeding her expectations. Solomon's preparation naturally commanded a reward; she gifted him 120 talents of gold, vast quantities of spices (never seen again in Israel), and precious stones.

Researching King Solomon's life and wealth creation revealed a valuable lesson for leaders: preparation attracts reward. Many leaders neglect preparation, failing to command results.

The Gem here is for leaders to constantly prepare, attracting remuneration and exceeding great reward.

- ◙ 153 -

A LEADER'S WEAKNESS

"King Solomon, however, loved many foreign women besides Pharaoh's daughter—Moabites, Ammonites, Edomites, Sidonians and Hittites. They were from nations about which the Lord had told the Israelites, "You must not intermarry with them, because they will surely turn your hearts after their gods." Nevertheless, Solomon held fast to them in love. He had seven hundred wives of royal birth and three hundred concubines, and his wives led him astray. As Solomon grew old, his wives turned his heart after other gods, and his heart was not fully devoted to the Lord his God, as the heart of David his father had been."
—I Kings 11:1-4, NIV

"So the Lord said to Solomon, "Since this is your attitude and you have not kept my covenant and my decrees, which I commanded you, I will most certainly tear the kingdom away from you and give it to one of your subordinates."
—I Kings 11:11

Like most leaders, Solomon had a weakness: women. He inherited this trait from his father, but his borderline obsession with foreign women was unprecedented. Despite warnings, he married women from nations the Israelites were cautioned against, holding fast to them in love.

Solomon's harem consisted of 700 royal wives and 300

concubines. This vast entourage did great harm to the wise King, leading him astray. As he aged, his heart turned after other gods, and he was no longer devoted to the Lord like David.

A leader must be self-aware of their weaknesses and prevent them from consuming them. Unfortunately, Solomon is now the poster boy for leaders' excesses regarding the opposite gender. His actions led to fragmentation of his heart and soul.

We see Solomon spending his latter days worshiping strange gods, leaving us wondering how much of himself he gave up for those he was chosen to lead.

- ◐ 154 -

EMPATHY

"So they sent for Jeroboam, and he and the whole assembly of Israel went to Rehoboam and said to him: "Your father put a heavy yoke on us, but now lighten the harsh labor and the heavy yoke he put on us, and we will serve you." Rehoboam answered, "Go away for three days and then come back to me." So the people went away. Then King Rehoboam consulted the elders who had served his father Solomon during his lifetime. "How would you advise me to answer these people?" he asked. They replied, "If today you will be a servant to these people and serve them and give them a favorable answer, they will always be your servants." But Rehoboam rejected the advice the elders gave him and consulted the young men who had grown up with him and were serving him. He asked them, "What is your advice? How should we answer these people who say to me, 'Lighten the yoke your father put on us'?" The young men who had grown up with him replied, "These people have said to you, 'Your father put a heavy yoke on us, but make our yoke lighter.' Now tell them, 'My little finger is thicker than my father's waist. My father laid on you a heavy yoke; I will make it even heavier. My father scourged you with whips; I will scourge you with scorpions.'" Three days later Jeroboam and all the people returned to Rehoboam, as the king had said, "Come back to me in three days." The king answered the people harshly. Rejecting the advice given him by the elders, he followed the advice of the young men and said, "My father made your yoke heavy; I will

> *make it even heavier. My father scourged you with whips; I will scourge you with scorpions." So the king did not listen to the people, for this turn of events was from the Lord, to fulfill the word the Lord had spoken to Jeroboam son of Nebat through Ahijah the Shilonite."*
> —I Kings 12:3-15, NIV

The ability to understand and share the feelings of another, which is the definition of empathy, is a secret behind the superheroism of many successful leaders. Leaders who fail to show empathy most often than not, always have themselves to blame, people want their leaders to genuinely care and be concerned, not to pay lip service but to be conscious of their emotional well-being.

King Rehoboam, son of Solomon and Grandson of David failed woefully in this regard and lost a chunk of the Kingdom of Israel. The men had approached Rehoboam asking for a respite, they stressed that his father had laboured the people with harsh conditions and heavy taxation to fund his grandiose infrastructure and luxurious style of living, they asked that if he gave consideration to their worries they would serve him, the young King asked them to go away to ruminate over their request.

At first, it appears that he does what is right by consulting experienced hands who served his father and they gave him good advice, telling him if he would be a servant leader and show empathy he would have the people faithfully follow him, but he also consulted his peer group who without wisdom and experience in handling empathetic situations advised him to do worse than his father, and even taunt the people that his little finger would be thicker than his father's waist and also if his father scourged them with whips he would do with scorpions.

Upon the people's return, he told them he would make their yoke heavier. This singular action would see the people resolve not to follow the house of David and will set in motion, the kingdom being divided and Jeroboam emerging as King over Israel, with only the tribe of Judah and Benjamin remaining, mostly because of God's promise to David that a descendant of his will always be on the throne.

The Gem here for leaders is to appreciate that they must never take for granted the feelings of those they lead, ensuring that they listen and genuinely appreciate the position of others is critical, Godly leaders must understand that God is conscious of our feelings and emotions, he shows empathy how much more us, Rehoboam failed to understand this and like it is said the rest is history.

- 155 -

TURNING A BLIND EYE

"Judah did evil in the eyes of the Lord. By the sins they committed they stirred up his jealous anger more than those who were before them had done. They also set up for themselves high places, sacred stones and Asherah poles on every high hill and under every spreading tree. There were even male shrine prostitutes in the land; the people engaged in all the detestable practices of the nations the Lord had driven out before the Israelites. In the fifth year of King Rehoboam, Shishak king of Egypt attacked Jerusalem. He carried off the treasures of the temple of the Lord and the treasures of the royal palace. He took everything, including all the gold shields Solomon had made. So King Rehoboam made bronze shields to replace them and assigned these to the commanders of the guard on duty at the entrance to the royal palace."
—I Kings 14:22-27, NIV

"Asa did what was right in the eyes of the Lord, as his father David had done. He expelled the male shrine prostitutes from the land and got rid of all the idols his ancestors had made. He even deposed his grandmother Maakah from her position as queen mother, because she had made a repulsive image for the worship of Asherah. Asa cut it down and burned it in the Kidron Valley. Although he did not remove the high places, Asa's heart was fully committed to the Lord all his life."
—I Kings 15:11-14, NIV

Kings or leaders who turn a blind eye to wickedness and injustice usually have painful endings filled with regret. After the kingdom split, king after king perpetuated evil in God's eyes, stirring His jealous anger. These kings ignored the proliferation of high places, sacred stones, Asherah poles on every high hill and under spreading trees, and temple prostitutes committing detestable acts that drove out the original inhabitants.

Specifically, in King Rehoboam's fifth year, consequences became apparent when Egypt's king attacked Jerusalem, carrying away temple treasures, including Solomon's gold shields. Every time a leader turns a blind eye, they invite a storm they can't cover from, losing divine protection and becoming prey to life's challenges.

In contrast, King Asa, who did what was right in God's eyes, like David, eliminated abominations and committed his heart fully to the Lord throughout his life. He had a good life, safe until his diseased feet at life's end. Asa is a leader worthy of emulation.

Godly leaders must never bury their heads like ostriches, ignoring surrounding issues. Leadership requires facing challenges head-on, whether palatable or not, and taking difficult steps to correct anomalies.

- ◎ 156 -

RELATIONSHIP LEVERAGE

"Let there be a treaty between me and you," he said,
"as there was between my father and your father. See,
I am sending you a gift of silver and gold. Now break
your treaty with Baasha king of Israel so he will with-
draw from me." Ben-Hadad agreed with King Asa
and sent the commanders of his forces against the
towns of Israel. He conquered Ijon, Dan, Abel Beth
Maakah and all Kinnereth in addition to Naphtali.
When Baasha heard this, he stopped building Ramah
and withdrew to Tirzah."
—I Kings 15:19-21, NIV

Leaders must appreciate the power of leverage especially when it comes to relationships. The Israelites were split into two Kingdoms, Judah and Israel and there were as expected constant wars between the two brother nations. Asa King of Judah and Baasha King of Israel had several confrontations and when Baasha would go up against Judah, he would fortify Ramah to prevent anyone from leaving or entering into Judah.

Asa was caught in a fix and had to take all the silver and gold in the treasuries and leveraged on an existing relationship between the King of Aram, emphasizing that similar had existed between their fathers, so as to win his support to fight Baasha and make him withdraw.

He would agree and send his commanders against the towns of Israel and when Baasha heard he stopped building Ramah and withdrew, leaving behind the stones and timber which Asa used to build up cities.

What is of emphasis and consideration is for a second imagine if there wasn't an existing relationship between the previous kings of Judah and Syria.

The Gem here is Godly leaders must never underestimate the power of relationship leverage, in many situations you may find yourself in, the only currency you may have to spend is relationships, it is for this reason it must be sought after, nurtured and maintained, as its use is certain, but the timing of that use is usually unknown.

- ◎ 157 -

NEVER LET YOUR GUARD DOWN

"Zimri, one of his officials, who had command of half his chariots, plotted against him. Elah was in Tirzah at the time, getting drunk in the home of Arza, the palace administrator at Tirzah. Zimri came in, struck him down and killed him in the twenty-seventh year of Asa king of Judah. Then he succeeded him as king."
—I Kings 16:9, 10, NIV

Many leaders that have been assassinated or removed from power, either in a bloody coup or maybe a bloodless board room conspiracy in some regards may have let their guard down. Those seeking to drag down a leader often wait till when the leader's guard is down and when he is most susceptible to attack without any response.

Elah, son of Baasha became King and one of his officials called Zimri who commanded half of his chariots plotted against him, it is recorded that while Elah was getting drunk in the home of his palace administrator, Zimri came in and struck him and succeeded him as King, killing off the entire family of Baasha mostly due to the sins they had committed and which eroused the anger of the Lord.

Whilst acknowledging that there was a prophecy to be fulfilled in this instance, leaders can learn that you become vulnerable when your senses are impaired, and when you are around familiar people because around strangers, senses will naturally be heightened.

The Gem here is that Godly leaders must never be in such a position that their guards are let down, whilst trust is a good quality to possess, it must never be a disadvantage, or something that can be exploited, regardless of the kind of leader you are always remember that the only person you can trust 100% is yourself, therefore never let your guard down.

- ◉ 158 -

BE CAREFUL OF
REBUILDING UP ACCURSED

"In Ahab's time, Hiel of Bethel rebuilt Jericho. He laid its foundations at the cost of his firstborn son Abiram, and he set up its gates at the cost of his youngest son Segub, in accordance with the word of the Lord spoken by Joshua son of Nun."
— I Kings 16:34, NIV

I am a firm believer in the what has come before sets the tone of what is to come, and it is why leaders must know the past to rule the present effectively. Hundreds of years after Joshua with his army had destroyed Jericho and God bringing down its ancient walls, a leader by the name of Hiel of Bethel arose to rebuild Jericho and maybe intentionally ignoring the prophetic words that came before or unaware he would lay the foundations of the city at the very pricey sum of the life of his first son or seed, and when he set up the gates, he also equaled the payment with the life of his youngest son.

Dear Leader do not wish this away as another Old Testament fairy tale, the Gem here is that Godly leaders must understand that certain actions can be akin to rebuilding the accursed things, whether physical or otherwise leaders must not resurrect unholy elements of the past, the consequences have far reaching repercussions.

- ◎ 159 -

SWINGING EMOTIONS

"Now Ahab told Jezebel everything Elijah had done and how he had killed all the prophets with the sword. So Jezebel sent a messenger to Elijah to say, "May the gods deal with me, be it ever so severely, if by this time tomorrow I do not make your life like that of one of them." Elijah was afraid and ran for his life. When he came to Beersheba in Judah, he left his servant there, while he himself went a day's journey into the wilderness. He came to a broom bush, sat down under it and prayed that he might die. "I have had enough, Lord," he said. "Take my life; I am no better than my ancestors."
—I Kings 19:1-4, NIV

Elijah was no doubt exhausted. He had just emerged from the Mount Carmel showdown with 450 prophets of Baal and 400 prophets of Asherah, who ate at Jezebel's table. It was the most talked-about event, with the people taking ringside seating to see if Elijah's God was far stronger than that of Baal.

The rules of the contest were clear: a bull was allocated to each team, cut into pieces, and placed on wood with no fire. Each side would call on their own god to send fire down to consume the sacrifice. The priests of Baal went first, crying from morning till late afternoon, beating themselves with whips and bleeding. But it seemed their gods were, as Elijah described, asleep or on holiday.

When no fire appeared, it was Elijah's turn. He repeated the ritual, taking it a step further by asking attendants to pour water into the trenches around the stone altar and upon the cut-up bull. Elijah prayed to the God of his covenant, and from heaven came a raging, consuming fire that not only burned up the bull sacrifice but also licked up the water and dust, obliterating the altar.

This feat gave Elijah the boldness and audacity to slaughter all the priests of Baal, bringing upon himself the wrath of the wicked Queen Jezebel. In a quick swing of emotions, he began wishing death upon himself, an event that would eventually lead to God taking him up to heaven.

As leaders, we must be wary of swinging emotions. During our journey, events will occur that make our emotions resemble a rollercoaster ride. There exists a wisdom to be applied; otherwise, the possibility of not finishing or not finishing well is real.

The nature of emotional awareness is critical for a godly leader. As a bundle of emotions, control is key. Swinging emotions may cause a leader to lose all and become prone to errors in judgment and discouragement, an emotion that takes much and gives nothing.

- 160 -

BURNING THE PLOUGH

"Elisha then left his oxen and ran after Elijah. "Let me kiss my father and mother goodbye," he said, "and then I will come with you." "Go back," Elijah replied. "What have I done to you?" So Elisha left him and went back. He took his yoke of oxen and slaughtered them. He burned the plowing equipment to cook the meat and gave it to the people, and they ate. Then he set out to follow Elijah and became his servant."
—*I Kings 19:20, 21, NIV*

There is a sound that a call of leadership makes. Its decibels and rhythm are almost unmistakenable and hypnotical in its operation when it rings in the ears of the leader.

This call often makes strange demands on those who are bold enough to answer and follow its leading into the unknown. One of those demands is burning the plow- in other words, taking a stand of not going back to the familiar past but instead trudging on to the unfamiliar future.

Elijah had just been given his final earthly assignments, one of which was to anoint Elisha, son of Shaphat, to succeed him as a prophet. He found Elisha plowing with twelve yoke of oxen. When the symbolic cloak throw was thrown, he understood what that meant. He requested to kiss his father and mother goodbye, then slaughtered the oxen and burned the plowing equipment. He threw a feast as he knew there was no going back.

Many leaders may face a variation of what 'plows' they need to burn- some might be certain individuals (not literal burning), some might be a few associations. Basically anything that serves as an anchor to keep you tied to the past and causes you to look back.

Elisha knew he would not carry out his full mandate if he still had thoughts of oxen on the field. He fell headlong into his new leadership position, and that is a sacrifice that must be made to be effective in your leadership assignment. The gem here is take stock of all those things and people who will be an impediment to you becoming a successful leader. Like Elisha burn them and move. So much awaits you, you will have no regrets.

- ⊙ 161 -

CODE FOR VICTORY

"Meanwhile a prophet came to Ahab king of Israel and announced, "This is what the Lord says: 'Do you see this vast army? I will give it into your hand today, and then you will know that I am the Lord.'" "But who will do this?" asked Ahab. The prophet replied, "This is what the Lord says: 'The junior officers under the provincial commanders will do it.'" "And who will start the battle?" he asked. The prophet answered, "You will."
—I Kings 20:13, 14, NIV

"Afterward, the prophet came to the king of Israel and said, "Strengthen your position and see what must be done, because next spring the king of Aram will attack you again."
—I Kings 20:22, NIV

The fallacy that most leaders rest on is that they hold the sole knowledge when it comes to the keys to be employed to gain an advantage while leading. It is the responsibility of any wise godly leader to seek out the code necessary to overcome challenges they encounter.

Ahmad was battle ready and a prophet came to him announcing his imminent victory, to which the king would question on what keys to unlock the doors to victory. He would be informed that though he may start the battle, it was the junior officers under his commanders who will see to the execution.

One can only imagine if he attempted to do this the other way around what the likely outcome would have been.

There is a code for every victory that you will receive, your job is to seek it out. A door is opened only with the keys that are suited to the lock. Discover the code and you will have a leadership journey filled with success.

- ◎ 162 -

CONTENTMENT

"Some time later there was an incident involving a vineyard belonging to Naboth the Jezreelite. The vineyard was in Jezreel, close to the palace of Ahab king of Samaria. Ahab said to Naboth, "Let me have your vineyard to use for a vegetable garden, since it is close to my palace. In exchange I will give you a better vineyard or, if you prefer, I will pay you whatever it is worth." But Naboth replied, "The Lord forbid that I should give you the inheritance of my ancestors." So Ahab went home, sullen and angry because Naboth the Jezreelite had said, "I will not give you the inheritance of my ancestors." He lay on his bed sulking and refused to eat."
—I Kings 21:1-4, NIV

The Bible speaks of contentment as great gain for all men, and leaders are not exempt from this injunction. Unfortunately, it is evident that those in authority seem to have greater desire for more, even when they have the world at their feet. (Remember David and Batheseba.) This is a snare that must be overcome. Unfortunately, King Ahab is another leader who couldn't grasp this, and there would be a ripple effect of divine punishment.

The King had sighted a beautiful vineyard belonging to a man named Naboth, close to his palace. He sought to make a purchase or even relocate the owner, so it could be used for horiticultural purposes. Naboth rejected the royal offer, informing the king that the vineyard was an inheritance. The King went home sullen and angry, like a little child refusing to eat.

While the following events reveal the consequences of the King's actions, leaders must never allow the seductive nature of the power they possess to rob them of the contentment and decorum expected from those who lead. You cannot have everything or everyone you set eyes your eyes on. Any rash attempt to use the scepter of authority to achieve this always leads to the leader's ruin, and there is hardly an exception to this fixed rule of existence.

The gem here is that leaders must be be content in all their ways. Every blessing you command comes from God above, and He does not delight in those He places over others to use such lifetime opportunities to convert what belongs to others. Be warned.

- ◌ 163 -

MISUSE OF POWER

"As soon as Jezebel heard that Naboth had been stoned to death, she said to Ahab, "Get up and take possession of the vineyard of Naboth the Jezreelite that he refused to sell you. He is no longer alive, but dead." When Ahab heard that Naboth was dead, he got up and went down to take possession of Naboth's vineyard."
—I Kings 21:15, 16, NIV

A continuation of the contentment gem brings us to when leaders misuse the power bestowed upon them. King Ahab had returned home to his bed, sulking about how, as the almighty king, he had been turned down by a mere citizen. At that moment, his wife Jezebel came in and asked why he was in such a pitiable state. When he ran through the timeline of events, she retorted, 'Is this how you act as King over Isreal? Get up and eat! I will get you the vineyard of Naboth'. This would lead to a serious misuse of power, a venom that must never run through the veins of the leader.

Jezebel then wrote letters in Ahab's name, placed his seal on them and dispatched the letters to the elders and nobles, requesting them to proclaim a day of fasting and have Naboth seated in a promenient place, and accuse him of cursing God and the King, so he could be stoned to death. This was carried out swiftly and evilly. When Naboth was reported dead, Jezebel informed Ahab to rise and take possession of the vineyeard.

Again the punishment was as swift as the action, leading Elijah to declare heaven's verdict on Jezebel and the House of Ahab. Misuse of power is prevelant in our common leadership spaces, whether visible or behind the scenes. Many leaders cross this rubicon without fear or worry, utilizing machineries and agencies to carry out their personal bidding, causing pain and inviting further wrath on themselves, when the repercussions appear.

The gem here is that godly leaders must never be seen to abuse the power. Compare this to King David's intent on possessing Araunah's threshing floor; he could have exercised power with little or no resistance but chose to purchase from his personal treasury instead. Avoid the urge to misuse power in any form, it often starts in subtly and unnoticeably. Be conscious always that leaders must give account—some here on earth and others both on earth and in heaven—on how they misused power.

- ◎ 164 -

SPOUSE

*"There was never anyone like Ahab, who sold himself
to do evil in the eyes of the Lord, urged on by Jezebel
his wife."*
—I Kings 21:25, NIV

Often, it is said that when a leader occupies the seat of authority, a shadowy character lurks behind the throne pulling the strings. In many instances, that character is the leader's spouse. With unbridled access to vital information, they have the opportunity to shape decisions and actions, even under the leader's nose.

When such a spouse or individual lacks the fear of God, it spells disaster when the leader's deeds are scrutinized. The revelation often shows that, due to their inability to rein in their spouse's excesses, they unleash another de facto leader on their people.

A spouse shares the most intimate and personal moments with leaders, influencing them when defenses are down. Their influence cannot be wished away, and leaders must be conscious of this. The account of Ahab illustrates this point, highlighting Jezebel's role in his downfall. Her sponsorship of his evil deeds was instrumental in his selling himself out.

Regardless of the label given to the influential individual in your life, the gem here is to never downplay their power and influence. Be wary of their leanings towards actions that propagate evil, for downfall is certain.

- ⬡ 165 -

ITCHY EARS FOR LIES

"So the king of Israel brought together the prophets—about four hundred men—and asked them, "Shall I go to war against Ramoth Gilead, or shall I refrain?" "Go," they answered, "for the Lord will give it into the king's hand." The messenger who had gone to summon Micaiah said to him, "Look, the other prophets without exception are predicting success for the king. Let your word agree with theirs, and speak favorably." But Micaiah said, "As surely as the Lord lives, I can tell him only what the Lord tells me."
—*I Kings 22:6, 13-14, NIV*

Leaders, more than others, suffer from what I term the "itchy ears-lie syndrome." This is a state where an individual is only interested in hearing pleasing words, giving no space to hear truthful ones.

Jehoshaphat, the king of Judah, visited the King of Israel, who questioned the ownership of Ramoth Gilead and proposed war against the King of Aram, seeking Jehoshaphat's support. Unwisely, Jehoshaphat allied himself with this venture and requested that the Lord's counsel be sought.

The King of Israel gathered 400 men to inquire from God about the course of action, men he knew would give pleasing comments to his itchy ears. Jehoshaphat asked if there was another individual to be heard from, and the King mentioned one, Micaiah, but admitted he hated him because he never prophesied anything good about him. The King had itchy ears, craving only pleasing words.

When Prophet Micaiah was summoned, he appeared before the kings, sitting on their thrones at the threshing floor by the entrance of Samaria's gate. The palace official informed him of his summon and the need to align with the other prophets' words, all predicting the kings' success. Initially, Micaiah played along but soon gave a damning prophecy, revealing the courts of heaven's happenings and how a spirit enticed the 400 men to deceive the King due to his itchy ears. Micaiah was subsequently imprisoned, with his release tied to the King's return.

As leaders, it's easy to be carried away and have ears closed to unpalatable words. Humility will ensure stability and prevent leadership ruin. Often, necessary caution comes wrapped in words our ears dislike hearing.

The gem here is: beware of itchy ears seeking only palatable words from individuals like the 400 prophets, who say only what pleases you. Remain open to all words and trust the Holy Spirit to guide you accordingly.

THE BOOK OF
II KINGS

- ◈ 166 -

LEADERS EAT LAST

"A man came from Baal Shalishah, bringing the man of God twenty loaves of barley bread baked from the first ripe grain, along with some heads of new grain. "Give it to the people to eat," Elisha said. "How can I set this before a hundred men?" his servant asked. But Elisha answered, "Give it to the people to eat. For this is what the Lord says: 'They will eat and have some left over.' " Then he set it before them, and they ate and had some left over, according to the word of the Lord."
—*II Kings 2:42-44, NIV*

This popular phrase in leadership conversations emphasizes how leaders must sacrifice and 'eat last'. It sets a positive tone for leaders who adopt this mantra, contrasting with the common expectations of taking the best for themselves and leaving scraps for those they lead.

Servant leadership is rare in our modern times, but history shows some leaders have embodied this unique quality. A gentleman from Baal Shalishah brought twenty loaves of barley bread, baked from the first ripe grain, to Prophet Elisha. With a heart full of love, Elisha requested that the bread be given to the people to eat, not stored for personal consumption. Despite the limited quantity for over a hundred men, he prioritized others.

Godly leaders never lose sight of this gem: the welfare and well-being of those they lead is paramount. They willingly sacrifice comfort to ensure others go first, demonstrating that leadership is a sacrifice and not a burden any random individual can bear.

To belong to the celestial class of leaders, live by the injunction: "let others eat first." Sacrifice endears people to you faster than anything else.

- 💎 167 -

FAITHFUL AND CARING
AIDES/ ASSISTANTS

"Are not Abana and Pharpar, the rivers of Damascus, better than all the waters of Israel? Couldn't I wash in them and be cleansed?" So he turned and went off in a rage. Naaman's servants went to him and said, "My father, if the prophet had told you to do some great thing, would you not have done it? How much more, then, when he tells you, 'Wash and be cleansed'!" So he went down and dipped himself in the Jordan seven times, as the man of God had told him, and his flesh was restored and became clean like that of a young boy."
—II Kings 5:12-14, NIV

Leaders should never position themselves so highly that they overlook the faithful and caring aides and assistants who can make a significant difference.

Naaman's story illustrates this point: two aides played influential roles in his healing. It was his maid who recommended that her leprous master consider visiting Prophet Elisha. Noteworthy is Naaman's humility, as a highly regarded army commander and valiant soldier, in considering his maid's suggestion.

Later, after meeting Elisha and being instructed to wash seven times in the Jordan River, another aide intervened. As

Naaman questioned the necessity of using the Jordan, his aide gently reasoned with him, pointing out that he would have undertaken a more daunting task without hesitation. Naaman listened, dipped himself in the Jordan, and was healed.

This mighty General submitted to the counsel of those in lower stations, who held the keys to his deliverance from the reproach of leprosy. Leaders must not dismiss the value of aides and assistants, who may carry answers to long-standing problems.

The gem here is: set aside pride and humility listen to these individuals, regardless of their lack of laurels and acclaim. They can bring solutions your way.

Look out for good and faithful assistants; they are rare.

- 💎 168 -

THE BLIND CANNOT LEAD THE BLIND

"And Elisha prayed, "Open his eyes, Lord, so that he may see." Then the Lord opened the servant's eyes, and he looked and saw the hills full of horses and chariots of fire all around Elisha."
—II Kings 6:17, NIV

A blind man will surely lead another blind man into a ditch, no matter how well intentioned such an individual may be. These were the words of Jesus Christ in one of His many parables. Many leaders are blind for various reasons, leading many institutions, organizations, churches and governments to disaster.

During King Aram's war with Israel, Elisha, like an undercover spy, would send messages to the King, revealing Aram's military strategies and movements to avoid certain areas. Enraged, the King summoned his men, demanding the traitor be identified. His officers explained that the leak was spiritual, and the eavesdropper was Elisha, who had access to their war rooms and bedrooms. Infuriated, the King sent a battalion to capture Elisha.

At daybreak, Elisha's servant saw the surrounding army and feared. However, Elisha showed no fear, declaring that their side outnumbered the enemies. He prayed for his servant's eyes to be opened, and immediately, the servant saw hills full of horses and chariots of fire. Elisha then prayed blindness upon the army, leading them into Samaria. After receiving hospitality, they were sent away, and Aram's raids on Israel ceased.

I ponder the alternative outcome if Elisha's spiritual eyes were shut like his servant's. Rash decisions might have been made. This scenario mirrors many leaders who, due to blindness, cannot lead their people to escape doom.

Godly leaders must possess a distinct vision range, giving them a unique advantage. This should be every valuable leader's stance: the blind cannot lead the blind.

- 💎 169 -

UNFAITHFUL AIDES/ ASSISTANTS

"Gehazi, the servant of Elisha the man of God, said to himself, "My master was too easy on Naaman, this Aramean, by not accepting from him what he brought. As surely as the Lord lives, I will run after him and get something from him." When Gehazi came to the hill, he took the things from the servants and put them away in the house. He sent the men away and they left. When he went in and stood before his master, Elisha asked him, "Where have you been, Gehazi?" "Your servant didn't go anywhere," Gehazi answered. But Elisha said to him, "Was not my spirit with you when the man got down from his chariot to meet you? Is this the time to take money or to accept clothes—or olive groves and vineyards, or flocks and herds, or male and female slaves? Naaman's leprosy will cling to you and to your descendants forever." Then Gehazi went from Elisha's presence and his skin was leprous—it had become as white as snow."
—II Kings 5:20, 24-27, NIV

Considering the previous gem on faithful aides and assistants, it's essential to acknowledge the flip side of the coin. Where faithfulness exists, unfaithfulness can also lurk, potentially tarnishing a leader's reputation.. The story of Naaman which we considered earlier illustrates this point. There is need for leaders to be conscious of unfaithfulness around them.

After Naaman was healed, he was overjoyed. He returned to Elisha's house, offering gifts to the prophet. Elisha declined, but Gahezi, Elisha's servant, was consumed by greed.

Wondering why his master would not receive rewards for such a notable miracle, Gahezi chased after Naaman's party, deceiving them into giving him talents of silver and clothing; keeping them in his house before appearing before the prophet. Upon his return, Elisha questioned Gehazi's whereabouts, and he lied. Elisha, aware of Gehazi's actions through spiritual insight, rebuked him, stating it wasn't the time to receive rewards. As a consequence, Elisha placed Naaman's leprosy on Gehazi and his descendants forever.

This story highlights a crucial gem: leaders must be aware of potential unfaithfulness among those closest to them. Many leaders have suffered consequences due to actions taken by their aides. Individuals like Gehazi can pollute and deface leadership, presenting leaders in a negative light. The lesson is clear: be cautious of those surrounding your seat of authority. Ensure they don't undermine your leadership.

- ◆ 170 -

MENTORSHIP COUNSEL FOR YOUNG LEADERS

*"Joash did what was right in the eyes of the Lord all
the years Jehoiada the priest instructed him."*
—*II Kings 12:2*

Joash was seven years old when he began to reign, following Jehoiada the priest's bloody coup against the wicked Athalia, Ahaziah's mother. After her son's death, Athalia had attempted to wipe out the entire royal family. However, the young prince Joash was whisked to safety by Jehosheba, Ahaziah's sister. He remained hidden with his nurse at the Temple of the Lord for six years while Athalia ruled.

When the time was right, the priest unveiled the new king, crowning Joash after taking sufficient security measures. Athalia was killed by the guards, Baal altars and idols were destroyed, and the covenant between God and the people was reinstated.

What strikes me is Joash's relatively young age when thrust into leadership. He wasn't the only one; time, chance, and destiny often propel individuals forward regardless of age or inexperience. This gem serves as wise counsel for young leaders.

Joash proved to be a successful leader, particularly in temple repairs, accountability, and administration. It's noted that he "did right in the eyes of the Lord" all the years Jehoiada the high priest taught and trained him.

If you find yourself in a leadership position with limited experience, it's crucial to identify a Godly mentor. They will guide and protect you from the vices surrounding leadership. Selecting such an individual requires intention and wisdom to avoid becoming a puppet to selfish desires. The gem here is: remain open to Godly mentorship, especially in unfamiliar terrain. Seek those who prioritize the greater good, with nothing to lose by telling you the truth.

- 💎 171 -

LEADERS- RESOURCES DISBUREMENT

"Therefore King Joash summoned Jehoiada the priest and the other priests and asked them, "Why aren't you repairing the damage done to the temple? Take no more money from your treasurers, but hand it over for repairing the temple."
—II Kings 12:7-12, NIV

The priests agreed that they would not collect any more money from the people and that they would not repair the temple themselves. Jehoiada the priest took a chest and bored a hole in its lid. He placed it beside the altar, on the right side as one enters the temple of the Lord. The priests who guarded the entrance put into the chest all the money that was brought to the temple of the Lord. Whenever they saw that there was a large amount of money in the chest, the royal secretary and the high priest came, counted the money that had been brought into the temple of the Lord and put it into bags. When the amount had been determined, they gave the money to the men appointed to supervise the work on the temple. With it they paid those who worked on the temple of the Lord—the carpenters and builders, the masons and stonecutters. They purchased timber and blocks of dressed stone for the repair of the temple of the Lord, and met all the other expenses of restoring the temple. "

I have stated that one of my favorite definitions of leadership is the management of humans and resources. Often, we tend to focus on the human element, subconsciously ignoring the importance of resources. Mismanaging resources can lead to utter ruin, not just for the leader, but also for those they are entrusted to lead.

The young King Joash exemplified effective resource management. He summoned Priest Jehoiada and the other priests, inquiring why temple repairs were stalled. He instructed them to suspend fund collection, previously handled by the priests, and instead, set up a transparent donation system. A public piggy bank allowed temple visitors to contribute, and whenever the amount grew substantial, Joash had his royal secretary and high priest reconcile the funds, demonstrating accountability.

The collected money was placed in bags and directly given to contractors working on the temple, eliminating middlemen. This efficient system enabled the purchase of necessary materials and expenses. Notably, this project had been stalled, and while I won't speculate on the reasons, it's clear that leaders must ensure judicious use of entrusted resources.

King Joash's approach highlights a crucial gem: leaders must institute measures to prevent corruption and ensure accountability in resource disbursement. There is no one-size-fits-all solution, but it's essential to prioritize transparency.

Godly leaders recognize their two-fold responsibility: managing both people and resources. Don't underestimate the importance of resource management; it's equally vital as leading people.

- 💎 172 -

ARROGANCE IN INSTIGATING BATTLES

"He was the one who defeated ten thousand Edomites in the Valley of Salt and captured Sela in battle, calling it Joktheel, the name it has to this day. Then Amaziah sent messengers to Jehoash son of Jehoahaz, the son of Jehu, king of Israel, with the challenge: "Come, let us face each other in battle." But Jehoash king of Israel replied to Amaziah king of Judah: "A thistle in Lebanon sent a message to a cedar in Lebanon, 'Give your daughter to my son in marriage.' Then a wild beast in Lebanon came along and trampled the thistle underfoot. You have indeed defeated Edom and now you are arrogant. Glory in your victory, but stay at home! Why ask for trouble and cause your own downfall and that of Judah also?" Amaziah, however, would not listen, so Jehoash king of Israel attacked. He and Amaziah king of Judah faced each other at Beth Shemesh in Judah. Judah was routed by Israel, and every man fled to his home. Jehoash king of Israel captured Amaziah king of Judah, the son of Joash, the son of Ahaziah, at Beth Shemesh. Then Jehoash went to Jerusalem and broke down the wall of Jerusalem from the Ephraim Gate to the Corner Gate—a section about four hundred cubits long."
—*II Kings 14:7-13, NIV*

Have you ever found yourself in a scenario where you instigated something with confidence, only to find yourself at the bitter end of it? Perhaps you underestimated the capacity of the person you challenged. This is precisely what Amaziah, King of Judah, did by instigating a needless battle.

Amaziah, buoyed by his recent victory over the Edomites, sent messengers to Jehoash, King of Israel, challenging him to battle. Jehoash cautioned Amaziah, advising him not to be arrogant and to enjoy his victory by staying home. He warned Amaziah not to seek trouble that could lead to his downfall and that of his nation.

However, the arrogant Amaziah disregarded Jehoash's wisdom and proceeded to battle. His army was routed, and he was captured. Additionally, a section of Jerusalem's city wall was broken down, leaving their defense vulnerable.

Many leaders, like Amaziah, become arrogant after tasting success. It clouds their judgment, leading them to take on more than they can handle. Sometimes, there's no justification for certain actions, driven solely by pride.

Such actions make leaders vulnerable and blindsided, operating on emotion rather than logic. In critical decisions like battle, corporate takeovers, business expansions, or competing with rivals, reason and fact must guide leaders to avoid defeat due to hubris.

The gem here is: Godly leaders don't get ahead of themselves; they lead with caution.

- 💎 173 -

OBEDIENCE

"Hezekiah trusted in the Lord, the God of Israel. There was no one like him among all the kings of Judah, either before him or after him. He held fast to the Lord and did not stop following him; he kept the commands the Lord had given Moses. And the Lord was with him; he was successful in whatever he undertook. He rebelled against the king of Assyria and did not serve him. From watchtower to fortified city, he defeated the Philistines, as far as Gaza and its territory."
—II Kings 18:5-8, NIV

The young 25-year-old King Hezekiah was a leader who understood the importance of obedience. His trust in God was legendary, that the records reveal that there was no one like him among all the kings of Judah, either before him or after him. He seemed to tick all the boxes by holding on to God, following His pathway, and keeping all the commandments that were given to Moses.

Whenever you go around seeking inspiration, don't look too far than this wise King who understood the correlation between when a leader is obedient, the results are usually predictable, which in this case the Bible says were successful in whatever he undertook. For emphasis, not once in a while success, but an all-the-time success. He was blessed with so much success that his rebellion against the King of

Assyria, which would have spelled doom, was a success, and in that same time, the twin state of Israel was defeated and led into exile.

His obedience would also lead him to attracting heavenly intervention when Sennacherib, the King of Assyria, would threaten destruction, and Jerusalem would experience a deliverance like no other in the face of annihilation. Godly leaders must never take for granted the role and importance of obedience; it may make all the difference in the journey of leadership.

Obedience, like most matters, is often down to a choice, to do things your way or to do things God's way, no matter how unconventional, foolish, or difficult it may appear. The result is usually one that never really weighs equally with the sacrifice that is put in. Whether the leadership role you find yourself in, you must endeavor to be the beacon of obedience to all matters of God. Let those you lead know your stance, and let the God of heavens see it and watch Him reward you for it.

- 💎 174 -

PUT YOUR HOUSE IN ORDER

"In those days Hezekiah became ill and was at the point of death. The prophet Isaiah son of Amoz went to him and said, "This is what the Lord says: Put your house in order, because you are going to die; you will not recover."
—II Kings 20:1, NIV

God clearly hates disorder. When I read about amazing leaders, it breaks my heart to see that, upon conducting a post-mortem analysis after they've departed the stage, nothing remains. Many leaders fail to take conscious effort in ensuring their house, either domestically or professionally, is in order. The truth is, whatever you don't intentionally undertake will be left undone – it's that simple.

King Hezekiah, as we've discussed, was an exemplary leader who showcased leadership qualities worth emulating. In his time, he became gravely ill and was near death. The prophet Isaiah was sent by God with a singular instruction: "Put your house in order" (2 Kings 20:1). Nothing more was said. Although King Hezekiah made intercessions, which God honored due to his obedience, granting him fifteen more years of life, God's instruction remains significant for leaders.

It emphasizes God's expectation for leaders to be mindful

of their limited time and prioritize preparing their affairs. I firmly believe leaders must operate with the consciousness of their brief performance window. At every point, the gem remains: be ready by putting your house in order.

Godly leaders should maintain organization and not wait for an exit notice, whether from the temporal or spiritual realm, before putting their affairs in order. This responsibility demands seriousness and diligence, not to be treated lightly.

- 💎 175 -

DISCREET WITH ACHIEVEMENTS

"Hezekiah received the envoys and showed them all that was in his storehouses—the silver, the gold, the spices and the fine olive oil—his armory and every-thing found among his treasures. There was nothing in his palace or in all his kingdom that Hezekiah did not show them. Then Isaiah the prophet went to King Hezekiah and asked, "What did those men say, and where did they come from?" "From a distant land," Hezekiah replied. "They came from Babylon." The prophet asked, "What did they see in your palace?" "They saw everything in my palace," Hezekiah said. "There is nothing among my treasures that I did not show them." Then Isaiah said to Hezekiah, "Hear the word of the Lord: The time will surely come when everything in your palace, and all that your predeces-sors have stored up until this day, will be carried off to Babylon. Nothing will be left, says the Lord. And some of your descendants, your own flesh and blood who will be born to you, will be taken away, and they will become eunuchs in the palace of the king of Babylon."
—II Kings 20:13-18, NIV

Today's modern world may conflict with this gem, but leaders should exercise moderation when showcasing their achievements. We see leaders' performances splashed across all media platforms, but wisdom dictates restraint in sharing accomplishments.

Envoys from Babylon arrived with a letter and gift, having heard of King Hezekiah's close brush with death. However, Hezekiah foolishly dropped the ball by showcasing everything in his storehouses. This prideful action would have grave consequences. He revealed all his treasures: gold, silver, spices, oil, armory, and everything else. Nothing was kept hidden.

When the Prophet Isaiah inquired about the visitors and their mission, Hezekiah naively mentioned everything they had seen. The prophetic word revealed that those same men would return and take everything back to Babylon. It's no wonder that when the Babylonians sacked Jerusalem, they knew exactly where to find everything.

The gem I hold strongly here is that there are seasons where leaders must be discreet with achievements. Not everything should be for public viewing, regardless of how esteemed the individual is. This is the undoing of many leaders who revealed too much information and paid the price.

Learn to keep some things secret. Even if you're exempt from the punishment of your actions, like Hezekiah was, those who come after you may pay the ultimate price.

- 💎 176 -

SELFISHNESS

"The word of the Lord you have spoken is good,"
Hezekiah replied. For he thought, "Will there not be
peace and security in my lifetime?"
—II Kings 20:1-9, NIV

Selfishness is never a good look on any leader. In my study, beyond Hezekiah's foolishness in opening up his nation's entire savings to strangers, the only other blot on what would have been an otherwise spotless record was selfishness.

Isaiah had just revealed God's mind to the King, clearly expressing His displeasure. Hezekiah was informed that not only would all the treasures be carted away, but his descendants would also not be spared; his own flesh and blood would become eunuchs in the palace of the King of Babylon. Yet, Hezekiah's response reeked of selfishness, saying, "The word of the Lord you have spoken is good." Why? Because, in his thoughts, "I will be long dead, and as long as I have peace and security in my lifetime, the entire country can go into exile."

Leaders must never act with tunnel vision, focusing only on the present. A leader's actions, like a pebble on a quiet pond, are capable of causing ripples through time. This is what Hezekiah failed to understand or appreciate.

A leader must not be concerned solely with the present and its immediate effects on their allocated space in time. They must be selfless, understanding the reverberating effects of their actions and having a heart of empathy for the consequences they undertake or fail to execute.

The gem here is: selfishness is a cancer that no leader should allow to infect their leadership. Do all you can to eradicate it. You are just a recurring decimal in a long mathematical equation; ensure you are remembered as a considerate leader who had one foot firmly planted in the present and the other stamped in the future.

- 💎 177 -

OFFSPRING

"Manasseh was twelve years old when he became king, and he reigned in Jerusalem fifty-five years. His mother's name was Hephzibah. He did evil in the eyes of the Lord, following the detestable practices of the nations the Lord had driven out before the Israelites. He rebuilt the high places his father Hezekiah had destroyed; he also erected altars to Baal and made an Asherah pole, as Ahab king of Israel had done. He bowed down to all the starry hosts and worshiped them."
—II Kings 21:1-3, NIV

We have discussed the role of spouses and children in our discourse about leaders, but it's shocking when a leader goes from hero to zero in the blink of an eye, and the offspring of an outstanding leader becomes someone who should be forgotten in a hurry. What was missed? What was ignored?

Manasseh became King at twelve years old and ruled for fifty-five years, doing immense evil in God's eyes. He rebuilt the very structures his father, Hezekiah, was celebrated for destroying, and even added more by worshiping the starry hosts. In fact, it is written that he committed more evil than the Amorites who preceded him, leading Judah into sin and prompting God to promise severe vengeance.

The question for leaders is: how do we raise our offspring to prevent such a drastic departure from our values in the next generation? Was Manasseh never involved by his father in the covenant and leadership responsibilities? Was he shielded by royal attendants and his mother, unaware of the burdens to come?

Leaders who appoint successors, especially from their own family, must understand their critical role in ensuring their legacy endures. They must prevent their life's work from being undone by an impressionable young successor unexposed to the real world.

The gem here is: keep your eyes firmly on your offspring. However, considering Hezekiah's attitude toward impending doom and his subsequent selfishness, it's difficult to escape the assumption that he cared little about his successor, even his own offspring. Godly leaders prioritize their offspring's upbringing.

- ◈ 178 -

TRUST IN PEOPLE

"Go up to Hilkiah the high priest and have him get ready the money that has been brought into the temple of the Lord, which the doorkeepers have collected from the people. Have them entrust it to the men appointed to supervise the work on the temple. And have these men pay the workers who repair the temple of the Lord— the carpenters, the builders and the masons. Also have them purchase timber and dressed stone to repair the temple. But they need not account for the money entrusted to them, because they are honest in their dealings."
—II Kings 22:4-7, NIV

Micromanagement by leaders has its own major drawbacks. Many leaders fall within this bracket and pay a huge price in return, often in the form of burnouts.

Josiah, the eight -year old King, demonstrated wisdom during his reign. He sent his secretary to meet Hilkiah, the high priest, to get ready the money brought into the temple of the Lord, collected from the people. As King, the discretion lay with him regarding the mode of operation, but he decided to trust people.

He instructed that the money be entrusted to those appointed to supervise and have them pay all the artisans. Furthermore, they need not account for the money rentrusted to them, because they were honest in their dealings.

I acknowledge that trust is a scarce commodity, and we cannot cast our pearls to the swine. Many are undeserving of our trust. However, as a leader, it is humanly impossible to do it all. Therefore, you must learn to trust people and take necessary steps to ensure that trust is not abused.

Trusting others frees up time for you as a leader to concentrate on leading effectively without being bogged down by details that can suck you into a wormhole. Josiah clearly trusted the contractors on the temple project because they showed a track record of performance.

The gem for leaders is to look for those who have been honest in their dealings and invest more responsibilites in them. Armed with trust, I have seen unlikely, unsung heroes when entrusted perform magic when the spotlight is on them. Not everyone is out to cheat or undercut. With the wisdom of the Holy Spirit, He will lead you on who to trust in your leadership expedition.

- 💎 179 -

CONFRONTING THE PAST

"Then Shaphan the secretary informed the king, "Hilkiah the priest has given me a book." And Shaphan read from it in the presence of the king. When the king heard the words of the Book of the Law, he tore his robes."
—*II Kings 22:13, NIV*

"Go and inquire of the Lord for me and for the people and for all Judah about what is written in this book that has been found. Great is the Lord's anger that burns against us because those who have gone before us have not obeyed the words of this book; they have not acted in accordance with all that is written there concerning us."
—*II Kings 22:13, NIV*

"Then the king called together all the elders of Judah and Jerusalem. He went up to the temple of the Lord with the people of Judah, the inhabitants of Jerusalem, the priests and the prophets—all the people from the least to the greatest. He read in their hearing all the words of the Book of the Covenant, which had been found in the temple of the Lord. The king stood by the pillar and renewed the covenant in the presence of the Lord—to follow the Lord and keep his commands, statutes and decrees with all his heart and all his soul, thus confirming the words of the covenant written in this book. Then all the people pledged themselves to the covenant."
—*II Kings 23:1-3, NIV*

The past is often viewed as a cesspool that no one ever wants to waddle through and because of this notion, I have discovered that we keep repeating the same destructive patterns that lead us no where, this is true for both the leaders and those that are being led. After Josiah would send Shaphan he would receive a rather strange book from Hilkiah the priest which was discovered in the temple of the law, it was the Book of the law and when it was read to the King, he tore his robe in agony, because he could on the spot identify what had gone wrong, he gave an instruction for his officers to make enquiries about what was written seeing that his ancestors had done great evil, upon getting a reply from a prophet, who spoke of the impending disaster that was certain. Josiah was promised that he would be safe from the doom because of his responsiveness and act of showing pain and remorse in front of his people, his tears were also accounted for. Upon receiving the news again, unlike his grandfather, he called all the people together and renewed the convenant between God and the people, all because he confronted the past.

As a godly leader, do not always run with the assumption that what is always behind is behind. It often finds a way to catch up with the present.

The gem here is that leaders must never be afraid to confront the past; by so doing there is so much healing that can occur and the corrections of past errors and mistakes will augur well for your leadership cycle and those who follow you.

THE AUTHOR

Chris Omoijiade, affectionately known as the CEO, is a dynamic figure whose multifaceted talents have left an indelible mark across diverse professional spheres. As an entrepreneur, engaging speaker, dedicated mentor, insightful coach, and innovative consultant, and minister, Chris' passion for teaching leadership and personal success principles has been the driving force behind his illustrious career.

He serves as the Chief Storyteller and Executive at TCOC Global, a boutique consulting firm dedicated to implementing effective tools for enhancing the value proposition and productivity of individuals and businesses. With over two decades of experience, Chris has conducted impactful trainings for prestigious entities such as Continental RE, Diamonds and Pearls, Etisalat, the Nigerian Army, Zapphaire Events, Corona Schools, and Wole Olanipekun & Co., among others, both in Nigeria and Internationally.

Chris' expertise spans management consulting, corporate training, and legal services. He earned himself a Bachelor of Laws degree from the University of Lagos and a

Master of Law in Telecommunications and Maritime Law from the University of Hertfordshire, UK. His skill set includes leadership coaching, personal effectiveness, success principles, strategic planning, people management consultancy, and emotional intelligence, catering to diverse clients locally and internationally.

In addition to his professional pursuits, Chris is a minister and a proud graduate of the Koinonia School of Ministry in Abuja. He holds a diploma in Theology and Ministry from the Remnants Christian Network-Adullam in Makurdi, Benue state. Active in esteemed professional bodies like the Nigerian Bar Association, International Bar Association, Institute of Directors, and Chartered Institute of Arbitrators, Chris is dedicated to both professional and spiritual growth.

Chris' literary contributions include insightful books such as 'Get Ahead: Practical Steps to Face Life's Realities and Embrace Success,' 'The Irrefutable Role of Gatekeepers,' and the recently concluded 'You Too Can Be Debt Free.' This latest work stands as a testament to Chris' personal journey as a debt survivor, reflecting his passionate commitment to empowering others in their financial freedom and journey into becoming the wealthy man whom God has designed them to be.

As the pioneer of Arimathea Believers Network, Chris envisions a ministry that raises and empowers apostles in the marketplace to seek and fulfill God's will. His desire to unleash the authority and power of God within the marketplace underscores his commitment to righteous apostles influencing and transforming the business landscape.

Happily married with two sons, Chris calls Lagos, Nigeria, home. His unwavering commitment to professional excellence and holistic development is evident in his active involvement in various professional associations, where he continues to contribute his expertise and leadership.

To book Chris for your speaking engagements, consulting, company keynote addresses, trainings, and for ministrations, you can use any of the channels below:

- +234 908 123 0000
- admin@tcocglobal.com
- Chris@chrisomoijiade.com
- Ceo@tcocglobal.com

Follow on social media

- chrisomoijiade
- chrisomoijiade
- @tcocglobal
- @arimathea_believers_network
- chrisomoijiade
- christopher Omoijiade
- The Chris Omoijiade Company
- www.chrisomoijiade.com
- www.tcocglobal.com
- www.arimatheanetwork.org
- comoijiade